960
MUR

Murphy, E. Jefferson

Understanding Africa

DATE			
FEB 21 95			

22725 BMS TUB

UNDERSTANDING
AFRICA

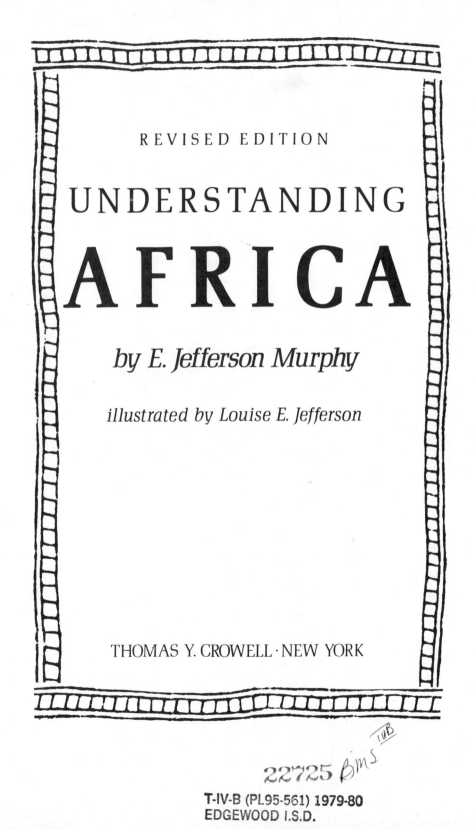

REVISED EDITION

UNDERSTANDING
AFRICA

by E. Jefferson Murphy

illustrated by Louise E. Jefferson

THOMAS Y. CROWELL · NEW YORK

LIBRARY OF CONGRESS CATALOGING IN PUBLICATION DATA
Murphy, E. Jefferson. Understanding Africa.
Bibliography: p.
SUMMARY: A survey of Africa, its geography, history,
population, natural resources, and cultures, with special
emphasis on the countries south of the Sahara.
1. Africa—Juvenile literature. [1. Africa]
I. Jefferson, Louise E.   II. Title.
DT3.M8 1978   960   77–11560
ISBN 0–690–03834–8 tr. bdg.
0–690–03846–1 lib. bdg.

2   3   4   5   6   7   8   9   10

To Millie,
without whose loyal support,
steadfast encouragement,
and constructive criticism this book would never have been
written.

By E. Jefferson Murphy

The Bantu Civilization of Southern Africa
History of African Civilization
Understanding Africa

Contents

Preface

This book, which grew out of twenty-five years of personal involvement with Africa and Africans, is intended to help Americans understand Africa better.

Africa is one continent—but a continent of many different peoples, each with its own history, culture, and language. Because of this diversity, "Africa" as a single concept exists more in the minds of modern people than it does in reality.

When one thinks of Europe, one thinks at the same time of the Germans, the French, the Italians, the Austrians, the Poles, and many other nationalities. But in the case of Africa, most Americans think only of "Africans." Americans have no historical contact with the

Ghanaians, the Kenyans, or the Zambians, much less with the Ashantis, the Ewes, the Fantis, the Kikuyus, the JaLuos, the Babembas, or the Barotse—to name only a few of the peoples who live within Ghana, Kenya, and Zambia.

Someday more Americans may learn to think in terms of the individual nations located in the African continent. But the modern world thinks of Africa as "Africa" —so we must start to learn about Africa in the same way.

Modern Africans themselves speak of "Africa." Although they are well aware of the diversity of their continent, they believe in African unity. From the far north to the far south, their common experience under European colonialism and common roots sunk deep in history have provided them with a point of view that overshadows many of their differences.

If we can keep in mind both the common traits and the diverse traits that make up Africa as a whole, we will have taken the first great step to understanding.

This book devotes its main attention to what is commonly called Black Africa—or that part south of the Sahara Desert. To most Americans, this is the least-known part of Africa. But the Arabic-speaking peoples of North Africa are of course Africans as well; and they and their lands are discussed in the book. The long history of contact with southern Europe and the Middle East has rendered North Africa unique on the African continent—but it is Africa, nonetheless.

UNDERSTANDING
AFRICA

Tunis
Algiers
Mediterranean Sea
Rabat
MOROCCO
TUNISIA
Tripoli
ALGERIA
LIBYA
EGYPT
Cairo
N

MAURITANIA
Nouakchott
Dakar
SENEGAL
GAMBIA
Bamako
GUINEA-
BISSAU
GUINEA
Freetown
SIERRA LEONE
Monrovia
LIBERIA
Abidjan
IVORY
COAST
UPPER
VOLTA
Ouagadougou
GHANA
Accra
TOGO
BENIN
(DAHOMEY)
Lagos
MALI
Niamey
NIGER
NIGERIA
CHAD
Lake Chad
Khartoum
SUDAN
Blue Nile
White Nile
REPUBLIC OF
DJIBOUTI
ETHIOPIA
Addis Ababa
SOMALI
REPUBLIC
Mogadishu
CENTRAL
AFRICAN EMPIRE
Bangui
CAMEROON
Yaoundé
Zaire R.
EQUATORIAL
GUINEA
Libreville
GABON
REPUBLIC OF
THE CONGO
Brazzaville
Kinshasa
ZAIRE
UGANDA
KENYA
Lake
Victoria
Nairobi
RWANDA
BURUNDI
TANZANIA
Lake Tanganyika
ZANZIBAR
Dar es Salaam
Indian
Ocean
Atlantic Ocean
Luanda
ANGOLA
ZAMBIA
Lusaka
MALAWI
Lake Nyasa
MOZAMBIQUE
Salisbury
ZIMBABWE
(RHODESIA)
NAMIBIA
(S. W. AFRICA)
BOTSWANA
Gaberones
Tananarive
MALAGASY REP.

AFRICA
Jefferson
SWAZILAND
SOUTH AFRICA
LESOTHO
Capetown

◄ 1 ►

America
Discovers Africa

In 1960, America discovered Africa. In that year, seventeen new African nations became independent states; and one of the seventeen, Congo, burst into flames as its army mutinied against the Belgian officers. After decades of relative silence, American newspapers carried front-page stories about events in Africa.

Before 1960, Americans knew little of Africa, although we were alerted to its "emergence" when the Gold Coast became the independent nation of Ghana in 1957. There had been exciting stories of Stanley's successful search for Dr. Livingstone in 1871. And we were briefly aware of Africa in 1935, when Mussolini's armies invaded Ethiopia and Haile Selassie bravely tried to defend his people.

Since 1960, we have heard much. Today attention centers on Southern Africa, where white minorities rule oppressively over black majorities. Angola and Mozambique, long ruled by Portugal, gained their independence in 1974, after years of armed conflict. But Africans still struggle against white rule in Namibia (South-West Africa), Zimbabwe (Rhodesia), and the Republic of South Africa (which many Africans prefer to call Azania). In many of the nations of tropical Africa recurrent military coups and grievous problems of drought and poverty remind us that Africa still faces momentous changes. Even Ethiopia is now under military rule, and is locked in combat with Somalia.

Americans have become aware of Africa through reports of these perplexing events, and we want to understand what they mean. But unfortunately, we have had little chance to get to know Africa well. We have to seek understanding of complex events by starting with uncomplicated analysis.

For hundreds of years, we have thought of Africa in stereotyped terms—and we are still heavily influenced by them. Our first task in understanding Africa is to look at our stereotypes, to learn why we hold them, and to try to gain a more accurate view.

Through Tarzan books and films, through the writings of early explorers, and from other reports we have come to think of Africa as a continent of jungle. There are, we imagine, towering trees that crowd out the sunlight, giant ferns, dank undergrowth, mysterious streams, pools inhabited by fearsome crocodiles, and a multitude of hanging vines.

Actually, most of Africa is desert or dry grassland. Only 5 percent of the entire continent might be properly called jungle. Even these areas are not quite as dark or impenetrable as they are usually portrayed.

Most Africans are farmers. They live in countryside not greatly different in appearance from the American West. Some Africans suffer from lack of water, and others from lack of wood; but few suffer the difficulties of the jungle.

Another idea derived from hundreds of adventure books and movies is that Africa is a vast preserve for lions, elephants, monkeys, giraffes, zebra, and other wild beasts.

In reality, the vast majority of Africans have never seen a lion, or any other large wild animal. Many Africans who go abroad see their first lion, their first elephant, or their first giraffe just as we do—in a zoo.

The majority of Africans live in areas that are not suitable for large wild animals. In any case the countryside is too thickly settled for wild animals to feel very safe. In East and Central Africa there are areas where wild animals roam, but these parts are too arid for people to live comfortably.

European peoples have thought of Africans as savages, who believe in witchcraft and superstition and live a primitive life. The missionary efforts of the past two centuries in Africa have almost always presupposed this condition.

Even the present-day desire to help the people of Africa is partly based on this centuries-old idea. It takes effort to remember that there are African scientists, engineers, poets, artists, and statesmen. And even then, many feel that these people must be the exception—that the outstanding Africans must be separated from the vast majority of their people by a wide gulf of education, ability, and special experience. This stereotype is based on the assumption that Africans have never developed any civilization, nor lived in highly organized societies.

The facts are remarkably contrary. Most African peoples have lived for a thousand years or longer in highly organized societies. There have been dozens of large African states, covering thousands of square miles, and extensive empires that rivaled Charlemagne's in area and complexity.

For centuries Africa has produced men of greatness. It has had in the past—and still has—a rich tradition of poetry, music, and sculpture. Africans are generally religious people; not only are there millions of Christians, and even more millions of Moslems, but native African religions are highly developed.

Africa has made some notable contributions to the world's culture. For example, American music, especially jazz, has been heavily influenced by West African music. Pablo Picasso and several other European artists credit West African art for some of their original inspirations.

These are only samples of the numerous stereotypes about Africa that the world has developed. It is important that we consider where these stereotypes began, and why they have been handed down.

The story begins with the Greeks and the Romans. Europeans depended on Greek and Roman writings for much of their knowledge of the world beyond Europe and Asia Minor, because Europe was isolated from the rest of the world right through the Medieval Age until the sixteenth century. Except for Marco Polo's travels to India and China, knowledge of the rest of the world began with the discoveries of Magellan, Columbus, Henry the Navigator, and others who explored late in the fifteenth century and early in the sixteenth.

Neither the Greeks nor the Romans knew much of Africa—except for North Africa, the country bordering the Nile, and part of the eastern coast. Herodotus, a far-ranging Greek, wrote glowing speculations about Africa, but his actual knowledge of the continent south of the Sahara Desert ended with Ethiopia. His map of Africa, drawn about the middle of the fifth century B.C., shows the Ethiopians (Abyssinians) living just below the Sahara, and nothing beyond but the "Southern Sea"—thus omitting the heavily populated portion of the continent south of the Sahara.

The Europeans had no real knowledge of most of Africa until the sixteenth century. They were buying products—gold, spices, Morocco leather, ivory—that originated in Africa, but these came to Europe via the Arabs. When the first European ships began calling at African coastal towns, the Europeans were not encouraged, by either the Africans or the terrain, to remain for long or to venture into the interior.

Thus Europe developed a steadily growing trade, but no knowledge of Africa. The great African states that were at their peak during this period were all in the interior, and remained unknown to most Europeans. Well into the eighteenth century, Africa continued to be only a name—a place from which useful goods (in-

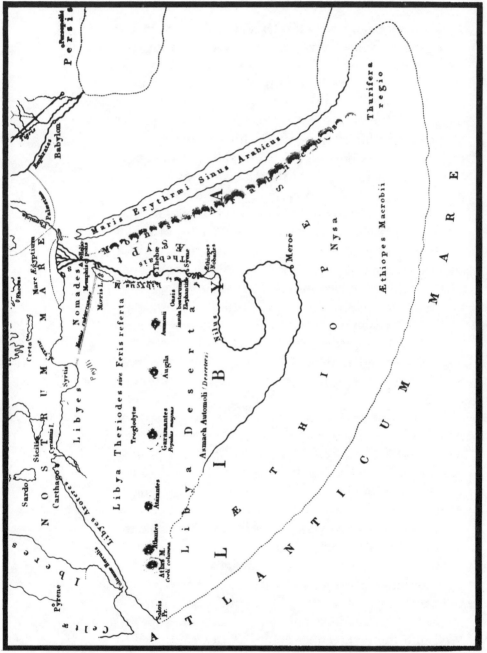

AFRICA ACCORDING TO HERODOTUS

cluding slaves) were purchased, but otherwise a mystery.

When the European explorers and missionaries finally arrived in Africa, they came with preconceived ideas. Africa was the "Dark Continent." Africans, known in Europe mostly as slaves, were ignorant savages, to whom the Europeans would bring salvation and light. There were Europeans who wrote home of the art, the music, the great states, and the wise kings of Africa. But there were many others who wrote of the ignorance, the disease, the superstition, and the need for enlightenment. Europe inevitably listened to the latter. Americans especially, burdened by a growing sense of guilt over the enslaving of millions of Africans, wanted to believe that Africa was a backward continent.

To these voices were added, in the late-nineteenth and early-twentieth centuries, those of European colonial officials in Africa. Their reports home often dealt chiefly with their own civilizing and pacifying activities, and little with the accomplishments of the Africans themselves.

Thus twentieth-century Europeans and Americans have thought of Africa in simple, stereotyped terms. And in 1960, when many African nations achieved independence, joined the United Nations, and began to receive worldwide publicity, Western nations were ill prepared to understand them.

Americans believe in the freedom of all peoples. We could not help but approve freedom for Ghana, then Guinea, then Nigeria, Togo, Congo, Tanganyika, and others—even if we had little understanding of what was involved. Americans were also disposed to be sympathetic to the needs of the African peoples as they achieved freedom. It was understood that they were poor and not fully prepared to cope with the modern world on equal terms. We accepted the necessity of aiding them. Western aid, though taking many forms, has inevitably concentrated on education.

Enthusiastically welcoming the emerging African nations and supplying educational help to them, Americans anticipated great things in Africa after 1960.

When, in the early sixties, the Congo fell into disarray, it was troubling; but the fault was thought to be insufficient education. Later, when Soviet influence was detected in the Congo, alarm increased. America realized for the first time that the Cold War could affect Africa. The military coups in several of the new nations, the development of one-party states with seemingly autocratic leaders, and further evidence of internal instability have not fitted original American expectations for Africa.

Consequently America's attitude has taken on a tinge of disillusionment. There have been harsh criticisms of America from several African leaders whom we once admired. There has been a growth of friendly relations between some African states and Communist countries. America has not been prepared for these developments. We do not understand them, because we do not understand Africa.

Over the past few years these and other events have produced a kind of "backlash" in this nation's view of Africa. Disillusioned with our role in Vietnam and perplexed by developments in Africa, Americans—though knowing more about Africa than formerly—feel they do not understand what has happened there.

New African states have tried to establish themselves in the comity of nations faster than their own resources could permit. They have experienced grievous problems; but at the same time they have achieved much. Americans hear of troubles, because troubles make news. Less is heard of the progress that steadily goes on: schools are built; agriculture is improved; roads are laid; industries are established; and nations are being slowly knit together.

To understand Africa better, we must examine the African past. But the first step is to look at the African land—because it is the physical environment in which people live that influences much of their history.

◀ 2 ▶
Geography of Africa

The most striking geographical feature of Africa is its size. Its 11,732,717 square miles make it the second largest continent on earth, after Asia. Within its area all of the United States, India, and Western Europe could be comfortably fitted. It is roughly three and one-half times the size of the United States.

Africa is bordered on its northern edge by the Mediterranean Sea. From its northernmost tip in Tunisia to its southernmost tip at the Cape of Good Hope, the continent stretches for 5,000 miles. At the Cape of Good Hope, the Atlantic Ocean is on one side and the Indian Ocean on the other. In a straight line from the Somali Republic's eastern coast, near the confluence of the Red Sea and the Indian Ocean, Africa stretches westward 4,600 miles to Senegal's coast on the Atlantic Ocean.

This enormous land mass has been virtually an island for millions of years—joined to Asia by only a narrow strip of land, which was "sliced through" when Ferdinand de Lesseps built the Suez Canal.

The northern coast of Africa, separated from Europe only by the Mediterranean Sea, has been close enough to share in the tides of history around the Mediterranean. Africa's northeastern corner, Egypt, has had a part in the great history of Western civilization that we know, and has helped to shape it for thousands of years. But most of Africa has been isolated from the Mediterranean world by the Sahara Desert, and from other parts of the globe by its own topography and by the Atlantic and Indian oceans.

Africa has been described, with some accuracy, as a saucer turned upside down. Viewed horizontally, its interior is a vast plateau, shelving off sharply to the sea. For example, the coastal strip at Accra, Ghana, is only about sixteen miles wide; behind it is a long escarpment, or cliff, which rises steeply to nearly 1,000 feet above sea level.

The narrow sea-level band that encircles much of Africa is dry and sandy at some points, marshy and moist at others. In western Africa, the interior plateau that adjoins the coastal strip is well watered, creating the great rain forests with their tall hardwood trees and dense surface vegetation. In eastern Africa, the portion of the interior plateau nearest the sea is dry scrub forest, with low, bushy trees and poor soil.

Inland in eastern Africa, a series of escarpments lead to ever higher plateaus with richer soil and cooler climates. Thus one finds in Kenya, farther inland and

higher than the first broad plateau, the lovely Kenya "White Highlands," which support a dense African population and have also attracted thousands of European settlers.

On the western side of the continent, proceeding inland, the great rain-forest plateau gives way to large, moderately fertile plains, or savannahs, which in turn border drier scrub forests. Still farther inland, these scrub forests eventually thin out and merge into the southern reaches of the Sahara Desert.

Africa's great interior plateau, south of the Sahara Desert, averages over 3,000 feet in elevation. Even when the coastal strip and the 3,500,000-square-mile Sahara (which has an average elevation of 1,000 feet) are taken into consideration, the average elevation of the continent is more than 2,000 feet above sea level.

Although much of this plateau is fairly level, it has notable contrasts in elevation. The Kenya highlands, covering thousands of square miles, lie between 5,000 and 10,000 feet above sea level. One drives across the equator, between the Kenyan cities of Nakuru and Eldoret, at an elevation of 9,200 feet. The Ethiopian highlands lie at about 7,500 feet in the west, rising to almost 15,000 feet in the east. Many of the highland plateau areas of Tanzania, Zaire, Zambia, and Zimbabwe are at elevations of 5,000 to 7,000 feet.

Most of the African plateau consists of vast savannahs, grasslands, and dry forest that lie at about 3,000 feet above sea level. Because these areas are near the equator, which bisects Africa, they tend to be hot and dry, whereas the highland areas are cooler and moister.

Africa has important mountains and mountain ranges. In northern Africa the Atlas Mountains, the continent's largest range, stretch in a gently curving arc nearly 1,500 miles through Morocco, Algeria, and Tu-

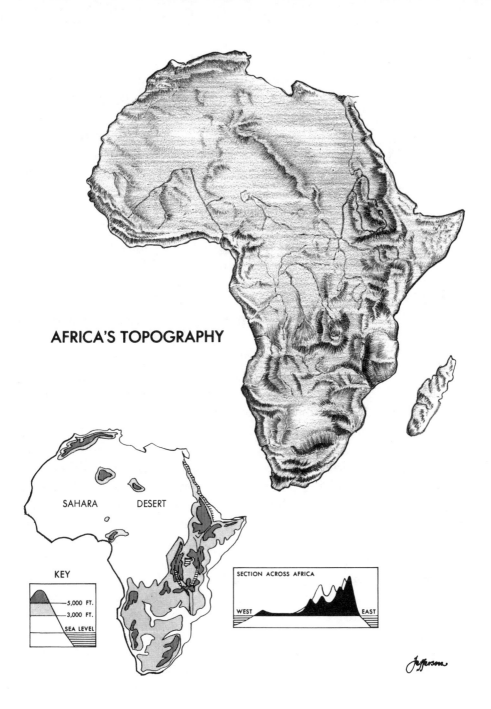

AFRICA'S TOPOGRAPHY

SAHARA   DESERT

KEY

5,000 FT.
3,000 FT.
SEA LEVEL

SECTION ACROSS AFRICA

WEST   EAST

nisia. The Atlas Mountains consist of three parallel chains that form the high northwestern rim of the African plateau. Mountains in the range rise to heights of nearly 14,000 feet, and their snow-capped peaks provide several popular ski resorts.

At the extreme opposite edge of the African plateau, nearly 5,000 miles to the southeast of the Atlas Mountains, is the spectacular Drakensberg chain. It rises to more than 10,000 feet in South Africa. The Drakensbergs form a long, jagged barrier between the coastal strip and the interior plateau.

From an elevation of 1,000 to 3,000 feet, the plateau descends to the sea along most of the Atlantic Coast of Africa. The plateau has few mountainous features. Moving southward along the Atlantic Coast, one comes upon low mountains in Guinea, Sierra Leone, Liberia, and Ghana, and inland in Nigeria. In Cameroon, the volcanic Cameroon Mountain, near the coast, rises to 13,353 feet. Other low mountain formations occur much farther to the south, in Angola.

On the Indian Ocean coast, no important mountains are found between the Drakensbergs and Ethiopia. But inland there are large mountainous masses, rising to heights of 7,000 feet, in Zimbabwe, Malawi, Zambia, and the countries of East Africa. In Tanzania is found snowcapped Mount Kilimanjaro, Africa's highest mountain. It is an extinct volcano with two peaks: Kibo, 19,340 feet high; and Mawenzi, 16,271 feet high. Fifty miles from Kilimanjaro is Mount Meru, which rises almost 15,000 feet.

Farther north, and still in the interior, is Mount Kenya, a magnificent, snowclad peak of 17,058-foot elevation; and, on the Kenya-Uganda border, Mount Elgon, 14,178 feet above sea level.

Perhaps the most romantic mountains in Africa, with

the possible exception of Kilimanjaro, are the great Ruwenzoris—the legendary "Mountains of the Moon." This chain, stretching between Lake Edward and Lake Albert along the Zaire-Uganda border, has numerous lofty peaks. The highest of these is the usually snow-covered Mount Margherita, 16,800 feet above sea level.

Ethiopia's great highlands are so marked by mountainous outcroppings that they are not true plateaus. Their level areas lie among impressive hills, mesas, and peaks that are often 8,000 to 9,000 feet above sea level, and that rise to 14,000 and 15,000 feet in some areas.

A fascinating feature of the African topography is the Great Rift Valley—a deep fissure stretching more than 3,000 miles from Arabia south through eastern Africa. Cutting into Ethiopia from the Red Sea, the Great Rift Valley is as deep as 2,000 feet and from 30 to 50 miles wide in most places. From Ethiopia it runs southerly through Kenya, Tanzania, Malawi, and Mozambique, finally flattening out on the floor of the Indian Ocean between Africa and Madagascar.

Lake Tanganyika, formed by the Great Rift Valley, is the longest and second deepest lake in the world. Eastern Africa's "great lakes" complex also includes Lake Victoria (the second largest lake in the world), Lake Nyasa, Lake Edward, Lake Albert, and Lake Rudolph.

Except for these, most lakes in Africa are small. Those that cover larger areas, such as Lake Chad, tend to be very shallow, with great marshy areas that fill with water in the rainy seasons but that are dry at other times.

Africa's most important and most famous river is the Nile. The longest river on earth, the Nile starts at Lake Victoria as the White Nile, winding for 4,160 miles through Sudan and Egypt into the Mediterranean.

The Niger, western Africa's mightiest river, flows 2,600 miles from the mountains of Guinea through Mali, Niger, and Benin, to form the great delta of Nigeria on the Gulf of Guinea. Also in western Africa are the Senegal River and the Volta, which has been dammed by Ghana to form a man-made lake of great size and importance.

The Zaire, once known to Europeans as the Congo, is Africa's second longest river and is 2,718 miles long. It drains a vast basin of 1,500,000 square miles, helping to create a densely forested jungle area in Central Africa that almost rivals the Amazon basin in size.

The only important rivers in southern and eastern Africa are the Orange, Limpopo, and Zambezi. Of these, only the Zambezi (1,600 miles long) is notable. Flowing into Zambia from the Angola-Zaire border area, it falls 343 feet at Victoria Falls. At the Kariba gorge, the Zambezi has been dammed to form the largest man-made lake in the world.

The subsurface of the African continent is composed of basalt—a hard, crystalline material that has changed little for millions of years. In other continents, volcanic lava has created fertile areas, or the advance and retreat of huge glaciers have pulverized the land surface to leave large areas of fertile soil. But Africa has few volcanoes and was untouched by the glaciers of the Ice

Age. Most of its soil is poor and shallow, composed largely of sand or metallic materials called laterites.

Because of Africa's geological history, it has few areas of highly fertile soil. The most fertile land is found on the high, mountainous plateaus, in the basins of the major rivers, and along the extreme northern and southern fringes of the continent. The soil of the Sahara is often fertile, but there is not enough water to support vegetation.

Dense vegetation, or productive agriculture, requires deep, fertile topsoil and a steady supply of water. Lacking these, Africa has sparse vegetation over much of its surface.

Let us imagine that we are standing in the center of the Sahara Desert, surrounded as far as the eye can see by shifting sands and barren, rocky terrain. If we go north, we emerge from the true desert zone into patches of grassland, olive trees, and small hardwood trees. Close to the Mediterranean Sea, we find wheat, citrus fruits, grapes, and cotton. Between the Sahara and the Mediterranean is a thin band of fertile land that stretches through Morocco, Tunisia, Algeria, and Libya to the Nile delta in Egypt. Since these countries also comprise part of the Sahara region, the people, animals, and vegetation all cluster in the fertile band near the sea or in the occasional oases in the desert.

To the west, the vast Sahara Desert extends through southern Morocco and Mauritania to the Atlantic Ocean. Only in southern Mauritania and northern Senegal is the Sahara modified by a few semi-fertile areas, where small, scrubby trees, wiry grass, and patches of vegetables relieve the barrenness of the desert.

But to the south and southwest of the Sahara, there is a fairly regular succession of extensive vegetation zones. The sand and rock of the desert shade off into a long, thin bank covered with tough, wiry grass and scrubby trees, called the subdesert steppe or Sahel. The Sahel, which is characterized by great heat and scanty rainfall, rims the entire southern edge of the Sahara, stretching from the Atlantic Ocean on the west to the Red Sea on the east.

The subdesert steppe is, in turn, bordered by a savannah, known as the Sudan, where the rainfall is slightly heavier and grass grows abundantly. In the Sudan appear taller and more luxuriant trees, especially farther south. The Sudan stretches from Senegal and Guinea on the Atlantic coast across to the Great Rift Valley and the mountains of eastern Africa.

Through much of Guinea, Sierra Leone, Liberia, Ivory Coast, Ghana, Togo, Benin, Nigeria, Cameroon, and Gabon, the Sudan merges into heavily wooded rain forests. The rain-forest zone stretches in a long, narrow belt along the Atlantic coast to Zaire, where it joins the larger rain forest of the Zaire basin that covers the heartland of Central Africa. The rain forest is a region of lush, dense vegetation that consists of tall trees, thick underbrush, and even, in some parts, of true jungle.

To the south of the rain forest of the Zaire basin is another wide savannah zone that covers southern Zaire, northern Angola, eastern Zaire, Burundi, and Rwanda.

Continuing still southward, the savannah blends into

BAOBAB TREE

sons, when the night temperatures run from 65 to 75 degrees and the day temperatures usually do not exceed 80 degrees. In many of the coastal areas, prevailing breezes ensure comfort even when the temperature runs in the 80's.

Africa's least comfortable climates are those of the deserts. Day temperatures in the Sahara can reach over 130 degrees, while night temperatures can drop well below freezing. The steppe bordering the Sahara also experiences high daytime readings, often exceeding 100 degrees, during most of the year.

In the densely populated areas, temperatures are normally not excessive. Cities like Accra, Ghana; Lagos, Nigeria; Abidjan, Ivory Coast; Kinshasa, Zaire; Dar es Salaam, Tanzania; and Mombasa, Kenya—all at or near sea level and close to the equator—are reasonably comfortable even for Americans and Europeans.

Africa's chief climatic problem, more serious than heat, is poor rainfall. Africa has about one third of the arid lands of the world. It has been estimated that approximately 60 percent of the continent's total area is arid, and that another 15 percent has scanty rainfall.

Much of Africa does not have enough rainfall to support high agricultural productivity. Of the areas that have an adequate annual rainfall, precipitation is heavy during part of the year and scanty during the remainder, which creates serious problems of water retention in the soil. Because of the poor soil composition, the water runs off during heavy rainfalls, carrying with it some of the topsoil and its valuable nutrients. This causes severe erosion problems in some areas.

It is sometimes said that Egypt has owed most of the tremendous agricultural productivity of its Nile Valley to Ethiopia. The rich soil of the Ethiopian highlands has for thousands of years been washed down the sharp slopes by heavy rains, into the fast-flowing Blue Nile. The loosened soil then descends the plateau into the Nile proper, to be deposited along the banks in Sudan and Egypt.

In West Africa the gradual drying out of the Sahara has created the semi-arid belt known as the Sahel. There droughts have produced widespread famine and loss of livestock. Large areas have suffered disaster, and there is little hope for improvement in years to come because of the light, unpredictable rainfall.

The human inhabitants of Africa have concentrated in areas where rainfall is good or which are near rivers, lakes, or waterholes. But water and a warm climate also attract insects and microorganisms. The former president of Ghana, Kwame Nkrumah, once proposed (not wholly in jest) to build a monument, in the capital city of Accra, to the mosquito. The monument would pay tribute to the historic role of this small insect in making western Africa unhealthy for European settlers. The European explorers of the eighteenth and nineteenth centuries, who returned to Europe racked with the fevers of malaria, could only portray Africa to their fellow countrymen as a forbidding land of disease and death.

The tropical character of the African continent makes it a happy environment for insects, worms, and microorganisms that threaten humans and many of the animals and plants useful to them. Yet people have survived in Africa for millions of years. Modern sanitation techniques, methods of insect control, and drugs for combating disease are gradually helping in the ancient battle against infection.

The disease-bearing mosquito, thriving in the tropical rain-forest regions and the heavily populated coastal strips, has made malaria a chronic problem. The mosquito also can carry yellow fever and elephantiasis. Although most Africans build up a resistance to malaria, it continues to cause many deaths. Those who survive bouts of this illness in childhood are often subject to chronic debility in adult life.

Most African nations have partially controlled disease-bearing mosquitos through improved water drainage, insecticide-spray campaigns, and chemical treatment of ponds. Relatively inexpensive drugs that protect humans against malaria are gaining wider distribution. Rural people are slowly learning to use them.

A variety of infectious organisms live in African waters, especially in sluggish rivers, ponds, swamps, and waterholes. In parts of western Africa, the Guinea worm causes painful sores, disfigurement, and often death.

In much of tropical Africa, but especially in the eastern and central portions, the disease known as bilharzia, or schistosomiasis, is widespread. This distressing affliction is caused by a small worm, which commonly uses the water snail as a host. The worm enters the liver, spleen, and other internal organs of humans who drink or touch the water in which the snail lives. Bilharzia frequently causes death, but even when death does not occur, the afflicted person suffers pain and serious loss of energy.

Also associated with a water habitat is the infamous tsetse fly. This insect carries sleeping sickness (trypanosomiasis) to both humans and livestock. Some areas of the African grasslands that would otherwise support a substantial population are sparsely inhabited because of the tsetse fly. And in other areas where humans have developed a resistance to sleeping sickness, no way has been found to protect cattle.

The tsetse fly can live only near certain kinds of vegetation that grow on the banks of streams. In some areas progress has been made by destroying the vegetation or spraying with insecticides, or even by catching and killing the flies. But this is a vast undertaking, and many other areas remain seriously infested.

Africa has traditionally been plagued by disfiguring diseases such as yaws, elephantiasis, and leprosy. Yaws has been almost eliminated in parts of the continent by a massive UNICEF campaign. Leprosy and elephantiasis are still serious in some areas, but medical practitioners have made appreciable inroads against them with preventive medicines, new wonder drugs, and health education.

Protective drugs are available that create resistance or immunity to most African diseases. It is possible to live in or visit most of Africa quite safely, if appropriate precautions are taken. Most cities in Africa have managed to exert significant disease control, including the provision of safe public water supplies.

Africa's diseases are a serious problem. Their prevention and cure are costly, and are not yet available to all Africans. Millions of Africans live in isolated rural areas, without the necessary drugs or the knowledge of precautionary techniques that could protect them. In the past fifty years colonial governments, medical missionaries, United Nations agencies, and Africans themselves have made great progress in the war against disease. The death rate for the continent has declined steadily. But the war is far from won, and one of Africa's chief problems is to ensure the health of its peoples.

African wildlife is the most varied and numerous of any continent on earth. In the greater part of western

Africa, larger animals live only in the remote interior where the rain forests give way to the grasslands and scrub forests. The wildlife in the rain forests themselves consists primarily of rodents, birds, snakes, monkeys, and diminutive antelope and deer.

The countries that have substantial populations of big game are Ethiopia, Kenya, Uganda, Tanzania, Zaire, Zambia, Zimbabwe, Angola, Mozambique, South Africa, and Botswana. Less significant big-game populations are found in Upper Volta, Chad, Niger, Central African Empire, Cameroon, and the far northern portions of the West Africa states.

Of the many species of wild animals, the elephant has been the most important historically. African elephant tusks have been the world's chief source of ivory for thousands of years.

Some of the first European trading posts established on the western African coast in the sixteenth and seventeenth centuries were attracted there by the ivory supply. Although elephant meat is eaten in some parts of Africa, it has never been an important food staple.

The African elephant is not as tractable and easy to train as the Indian elephant; therefore it has rarely been used for work. Some ingenious Belgians established a "school" in the Congo to train baby elephants to pull timber, but this is an interesting exception to the rule.

Lions are found in many parts of Africa, along with hyenas, leopards, wild dogs, jackals, and foxes. On the great plains of eastern Africa, these flesh-eating animals prey on herds of wildebeests, antelopes, gazelles, and zebras. But they are not a serious danger to the human populations of the area.

Africa's herds of antelopes and other herbivores have long been a source of food for Africans—but not a major one. Leading authorities on wildlife now advocate planned "game cropping" and controlled slaughter in order to develop a permanent meat supply from these herds, but no major programs to accomplish this have yet been undertaken.

Tourists and hunters have been attracted to Africa for its big game. Over the past few decades many African governments have recognized the economic importance of their game and have established a number of national parks and game preserves. Some of these preserves, such as the huge Serengeti National Park in Tanzania, are difficult to reach; but others, like Kenya National Park near Nairobi, are easily accessible.

At Kenya National Park it is possible to drive slowly along the roads in a taxi and see wild elephants, giraffes, zebras, rhinos, lions, and many other species, with the gleaming skyscrapers of the city of Nairobi in the background. Busloads of young African schoolchildren eagerly crane out of the windows to see an elephant or a lion for the first time.

Murchison National Park, in northern Uganda, has the largest concentration of elephants in the world. It is estimated that the elephant population currently there exceeds 20,000.

Kenya's capital of Nairobi, and Arusha, in Tanzania, are the safari centers of Africa. In both cities are firms that offer a guided safari (a Swahili word meaning "a trip") to hunt or photograph game in romantically wild areas. Happily for the game supply, and for Africa's future economic prosperity, the safari trend is toward photographing game, and away from hunting it. The urge to see wild tropical animals in their natural habitat is strong, especially for Americans and Europeans. Increasingly Africans, too, are drawn as tourists to see the great game preserves of eastern and central Africa.

The greatest resource of the African continent lies in

its mineral deposits. Even though large areas have not been explored geologically, Africa already produces significant proportions of the world's supply of certain metals, minerals, and gems.

Roughly 97 percent of the entire world's supply of diamonds, of both gem and industrial quality, comes from Africa. The major source is the great mines of South Africa; but important quantities of diamonds also come from Guinea, Sierra Leone, Ghana, Zaire, Angola, and Tanzania.

Gold is another resource that has long been exploited. Africa produces slightly more than half the world's gold supply from mines in South Africa, Ghana, and several other countries.

Approximately 23 percent of the world's copper comes from the rich Copper Belt of Zambia and Zaire. Zambia alone often ranks as the second- or third-largest copper exporter in the world, rivaling the United States and the Soviet Union.

Although the African continent contains much iron ore, it does not mine enough to rank as an important iron producer. The reason is partly the low quality of the iron ore and partly the fact that some of the richer ores are in isolated areas. Liberia, which has exceptionally rich iron deposits, now produces significant quantities. Iron is being commercially exploited in the countries of North Africa and in Mauritania, Guinea, Sierra

Leone, Angola, Zimbabwe, and the Republic of South Africa; and large reserves are known to exist in Nigeria, Gabon, Zaire, and Swaziland.

In addition to diamonds, gold, copper, and iron, Africa's share of world production of several other minerals is impressive: cobalt (76 percent), chromite (34.5 percent), lithium (98 percent), beryl (40 percent), kyanite (68 percent), manganese (22 percent), vanadium (30 percent), antimony (22 percent), platinum (30 percent), phosphates (26 percent), and vermiculite (25 percent). Bauxite is now in significant production in Guinea, Ghana, and Cameroon. With the great hydroelectric potential of these countries, this mineral promises to become a very important source of wealth.

In order to obtain value from mineral resources, there are four basic necessities: (1) money for equipment and skilled workers; (2) a sound knowledge of modern mining techniques; (3) good transportation to convey the ore, minerals, or refined metals to the sea for export; and (4) plentiful, reasonably priced energy sources. Of these four necessities, money can be at-

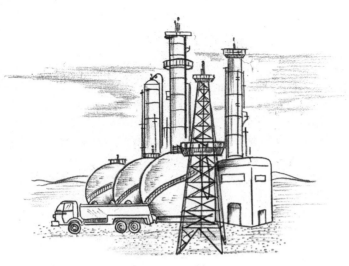

tracted from foreign sources, skilled technicians can be recruited or trained, and even transportation facilities can be constructed; but low-cost energy sources must first be present near the mineral deposits.

In the past, energy for most mining has come from coal, natural gas, or oil. Africa's coal deposits are relatively small. South Africa and Zimbabwe have been Africa's chief coal producers. Deposits of coal are known to exist in Mozambique, Tanzania, and Zambia; but only Zambia is beginning to mine them. In recent years Africa has begun to produce large quantities of oil; Angola, Algeria, Libya, and Nigeria are the most important oil-producing countries. Nigeria was in 1975 the second-largest supplier of oil to the United States.

The unique "upside-down saucer" shape of Africa, with its rivers tumbling from the plateau to the sea, gives the continent a vast hydroelectric potential. Africa is estimated to have 40 percent of the hydroelectric potential of the world. In recent years several countries have built great dams that generate enormous power.

Ghana has the Akosombo Dam; Zambia and Zimbabwe the Kariba Dam; and Egypt the Aswan Dam. Ghana's Akosombo Dam generates approximately 883,000 kilowatts of electricity—or six times the 1965 electrical output of the country. Smaller, but important, dams are being planned or are under construction in several other countries.

In addition to its hydroelectric potential, Africa has important deposits of uranium and other fissionable raw materials, which someday will supply nuclear power plants. Only Zaire and South Africa mine these materials now; but Nigeria, Zambia, Mozambique, Gabon, Madagascar, and Senegal also are known to have deposits.

Over 75 percent of Africa's people are engaged in subsistence or commercial agriculture. Most African farmers practice subsistence farming; that is, they produce what they and their families need to live on, with little extra to sell for income. In much of Africa the soil is not sufficiently fertile nor the farming techniques adequate to grow a large surplus for sale. In other areas the soil is best suited to certain crops, such as yams, cassava, and plantains, which have little market value outside those areas.

In the rain-forest regions of western and central Africa, the typical farm and garden staples are yams, cassava, plantains, bananas, and manioc. Yams, cassava, and manioc are root crops, while bananas and plantains are fruits. All are high in carbohydrate content, providing a valuable starch base for the African diet. The farmers also produce (usually from small gardens) tomatoes, onions, peppers, and various leafy greens, such as spinach and collards.

In the great savannah areas, grains—chiefly millet, sorghum, and corn—are cultivated, while from garden patches come the same vegetables: tomatoes, onions, peppers, and greens.

In the plateau areas of eastern, central, and southern Africa, corn is the major grain, although millet is also found. Bananas are important diet staples in the coastal areas and in some of the highlands of Tanzania, Kenya, and Uganda.

The coastal areas of the African continent produce a variety of tropical fruits: bananas, citrus fruits, mangoes, pineapples, and avocados.

Where cash products are produced in Africa, the plantation system or other highly organized methods of labor are often depended upon. This has been traditional in farming such products as rubber in Liberia, sugar in Uganda, cocoa in Zaire, and sisal (from the fibers of which rope is made) in Tanzania. However, African farmers have begun to grow on their own land important cash crops for sale: cocoa in Ghana; palm oil (extracted from the fruit of certain palms), for use in cooking and in soap manufacture, in Nigeria; coffee in Kenya and Tanzania; and, increasingly, rubber in Liberia.

The tsetse fly has prevented cattle raising in parts of Africa. In most areas where cattle can be kept, the grasses are not of a quality to make them fat enough for export. Africa has roughly 12 percent of the world's cattle, and many countries do list cowhide as an important export. But milk is in short supply almost everywhere, and many African countries must import meat.

Goats, sheep, and chickens are found throughout Africa, and serve as important meat sources. But these animals, like cattle, are unprofitable for export.

Africa does produce a major share of the world's supply of some agricultural commodities. Nearly the entire world's supply of vanilla and cloves comes from

Africa, as do over 75 percent of all the world's cocoa, over 80 percent of the palm oil and palm kernels, and nearly 70 percent of the sisal. Cotton production is important in Africa, especially in Egypt, Sudan, and Uganda. Roughly one fourth of all the peanuts consumed in the world are grown in Africa, with Senegal, Gambia, Nigeria, and Mali the most important producers. Other notable African agricultural products are olive oil, wine, sesame seeds, castor beans, coffee, tobacco, and tea.

For many years to come, Africa will depend on farm products as its chief means of livelihood. In its present pattern of agriculture, however, Africa faces two key problems.

First, most African farmers achieve very low yields. They work hard and have developed remarkably sound farming techniques to produce crops in poor soil. But, in addition to the poor quality of the soil, the water supplies are inadequate. Heavy rains may fall at one time of the year only, with no rain for the rest of the year.

If African farmers are to achieve higher yields, it will be necessary to apply the best scientific and technological knowledge available. Irrigation is needed, as well as better fertilizers. Crop research must find better, hardier plants that will thrive and bring high yields under African growing conditions. And peasant farmers must learn to abandon their time-tested crops and techniques when better ones are found.

The second problem is that many countries depend entirely on one crop or a few crops for their farm income. Cocoa in Ghana, rubber in Liberia, palm oil and peanuts in Nigeria, sisal and cloves in Tanzania—the income of these countries goes up and down sharply as world prices for their chief crops rise or fall. When the

CACAO PODS (COCOA)

costs of government, the building of schools, and the development of welfare services depend on income from one or a few crops, African countries have difficulties in planning ahead.

African leaders are deeply concerned over their agricultural problems, for it will take large sums of money and highly skilled scientists and technicians to find the right answers.

There are a few parts of Africa in which forest products are sources of income, as well as providing wood for furniture and fires. Along the rain-forest coast of western Africa, from Guinea down to Zaire, lumbering is increasingly important. Wood products are major exports of Ghana and Gabon, for example, while the sap or fruits of some trees, such as cocoa, palm oil, and rubber, are responsible for much of the national income of Liberia, Ivory Coast, Ghana, Togo, Benin, and Nigeria.

In eastern and central Africa, on the high plateaus, large companies as well as small farmers have planted whole forests that yield wood or bark products—such as wattle, which furnishes an extract used in tanning leather. In Mozambique and Tanzania are commercially valuable forest areas that supply cashew fruits (the kernels of which are familiar to us as cashew nuts) and cloves.

Fishing on the seacoasts of the African continent, as well as on most of the rivers and inland lakes, has traditionally provided food. In some places the coastal inhabitants take large enough catches to sell dried fish to people inland. Commercial-fishing explorations from a number of European countries have discovered important new fishing grounds off Africa's coasts, where tuna, herring, and sardines can be caught in plentiful quantities. Several African countries are building diesel fishing craft, freezing plants, and canneries to capitalize on their offshore fishing grounds.

In addition to developing commercial fishing in offshore waters, a number of African countries are breeding fish to stock their lakes, rivers, and ponds. These governments are helping farmers to build small dams and ponds for this purpose. Freshwater fishing is increasingly important in eastern and central Africa due to fish-stocking programs and better fishing methods.

Africa's terrain ranges from scorched desert to dank rain forest, from low coastal flats to high mountain plateaus. Yet people inhabit the entire continent—even the desert—and have learned how to earn a living from the land and the sea.

The agriculture of Africa, primitive though it may appear to the modern American farmer, is surprisingly effective in terms of the soil, water, insect, and climatic conditions of the area. American farmers may grow huge yields of corn and wheat in the fertile, well-watered Midwest; but African farmers must do the best they can with poorer soils, hotter climates, and less water.

Those who do not understand this about Africa often seek overly simple solutions. It is said, for example, that if African farmers had more plows, they could produce far more. The fact is that in many parts of Africa, plows would cut so deeply into the thin topsoil that it would erode and wash away with the next heavy rain.

Africans are well adapted to their environment. Their

primary problems are not learning to plant better crops and use better equipment. Rather, they must solve harsher problems: how to attain high yields in soil that is poor, how to preserve shallow topsoils from exhaustion, how to retain water supplies when rainfall is irregular, how to prevent heavy rains from inundating farms and eroding the soil, how to protect crops and livestock from dangerous insects.

◄ 3 ►

The People
and Nations of Africa

Only in the past few years have African countries managed to develop a reliable census system. In parts of Africa, census figures are only estimates. When the reliable census figures and the estimates are pieced together, Africa can be said to have 400 million people. This population—a small one for so large an area—includes not only the "real" Africans but some millions of immigrants from Europe, Asia, and Asia Minor.

The peoples of Africa are very diverse. They range in physical appearance from the dark-skinned Negroes of West Africa, through the lighter-skinned Caucasoids of North Africa, to the fair-skinned European descendants of South Africa. They include such people as the Twa, whom whites call Pygmies, and Khoisan, whom whites call Bushmen. They are like no other groups on earth.

These peoples speak more than eight hundred different languages, often as different from one another as English is from Turkish.

In culture, too, they are quite diverse. There are still small bands of Khoisan who depend wholly on hunting and gathering for their meager living. But in Ghana and Nigeria millions of people live in cultures rich in history and art. And there are the Egyptians, the Ethiopians, and the Sudanese, who can trace their lineages back to the very dawn of world civilization.

We think of Africans as dark-skinned Negroes—as indeed many Africans are. But racial characteristics are not very helpful in describing any people. This is partly because race has little or nothing to do with the way a people talk, or worship, or build, or think, or make their living, and partly because it is very difficult to measure racial characteristics with any precision. To describe Africa's peoples, we must think not only in terms of race but also in terms of language, history, and culture.

Africans are many peoples, and yet they share some common characteristics. These characteristics stem in part from the domination of Africa by Europe for the past few centuries. They include a sense of having been victimized by the huge trade in slaves and by colonialism; a feeling of being "poor" in an affluent world; and a sense of being set apart, by racial and historical differences, from the peoples of Europe.

MASAI MAN

More importantly, Africans also share a common cultural base—a fact only recently understood by anthropologists and historians. In the Old Stone Age period of human development, there was a culture—a way of life, of thought, of making a living—that was common to both Europeans and Africans. But more than ten thousand years ago, the two great cultural traditions, European and African, diverged into separate paths of development. It was much later that the African tradition split again into many various branches. Just as an Englishman and a Spaniard speak different languages yet share common roots, so the Ewe and the Kikuyu, the Baluba and the Wolof share common sources of language, culture, and history.

Africa is correctly called "the birthplace of man." The earliest known human relics have been unearthed there. In fact, most authorities now believe that man originated in Africa, then migrated to other continents. Dr. Louis S. B. Leakey, a noted scholar from Kenya, found animal bones and stone artifacts that indicate the existence of "human" types in Kenya perhaps a million and a half years ago. The bones discovered by Dr. Leakey are somewhat similar to bones, dating from a slightly more recent age, that were found in South Africa by Dr. Raymond Dart and Mr. Robert Broom. The remains from Kenya were found buried among quantities of crudely chipped stone tools. This indicates that the bones are those of a creature that used its mind and its hands to create tools. It probably looked as much like an upright ape, walking on two legs, as like a human. But it was human in that it made tools. Dr. Leakey gave it the name Zinjanthropus.

More recently Dr. Leakey's son, Richard, and other scientists have found skulls and skeletal fragments more than 3,000,000 years old, and clearly ancestral to modern man. All these finds, together with the countless ancient stone tools that abound in Africa, show a long line of evolution from primitive humanlike creatures up to modern man. Nowhere else on earth is there such abundant evidence of human origin and development.

With the modern concern about the "population explosion," it is difficult to realize that people once existed in very small numbers. About eight thousand years ago, Africa like other parts of the world was populated by small bands of people. These groups roamed large areas, hunting wild animals for food, or lived in small settlements along the seacoasts, lakes, and rivers, depending on fish for their main diet.

Africans of eight thousand years ago were probably divided into several general racial groups, with a good deal of intermixture taking place—as it had before and has since. In the southern part of the continent were mainly short-statured peoples, yellowish in skin color, who were the ancestors of the Khoisan peoples whom whites later called "Bushmen" and "Hottentots." These Khoisan peoples may have at one time spread over most of the African continent and then been gradually absorbed by other peoples. In northern Africa the lighter-skinned Caucasoids of the Mediterranean Coast had probably begun to mix with other racial strains to form the ancestors of today's Berbers, Egyptians, Ethiopians, and Somalis. In the Sahara the people may have been more similar to the Negroid peoples of today's West Africa and East Africa; they inhabited a huge area including much of central Africa. These people seem to have had a considerable effect, both racially and culturally, in the development of most of the modern peoples of Africa.

In the Africa of eight thousand years ago, the Sahara was a relatively well-watered prairie, with a number of rivers and a substantial rainfall. Fairly large settlements had been established along the rivers by fisher peoples. They were spread thinly from near the Mediterranean southward to the dense forests of western Africa. Then, about five thousand years ago, the Sahara slowly began

to dry out. As it became less hospitable, its peoples migrated to the north and to the south.

In these migrations the Negroid peoples of the Sahara, who may have already begun to practice the cultivation of grain, influenced the peoples of the Mediterranean coast and intermarried with them in many areas. But it was to the east and the south that their main influence was felt.

Migrating east, the Saharan Negroid peoples helped to launch the great Egyptian civilization of the Nile Valley. There is clear archeological evidence of their influence dating from about 5000 B.C. Whether the Saharans brought agriculture to the Nile Valley or whether it was borrowed by the Egyptians from the ancient peoples of the Middle East (the lands described in the Bible) is unclear. But the Egyptian civilization developed rapidly after the arrival of the Negroid Saharan peoples. By 4000 B.C. cities had been founded, a calendar developed, and hieroglyphic writing was being used. And by 3400 B.C., all Egypt was united into one great kingdom, which was the most resplendent on earth.

Moving south after about 5000 B.C., the ancient Saharans intermixed with the indigenous peoples of the western and southern Sudan, forming the Negroid groups who later developed the great empires that held sway in that region. They began to practice agriculture sometime between 4000 B.C. and 1000 B.C., and appear to have begun organizing into kingdoms soon after 1000 B.C.

Still other Saharan groups apparently moved southeast into Nubia and Ethiopia, there to form groups that developed somewhat differently from their cousins in western Africa. But in eastern Africa they also eventually developed agriculture and formed kingdoms, between 2000 and 1000 B.C.

The southward migrations continued until recent times. By the time of Christ the Negroid peoples of western Africa had crossed the great rain forests of Zaire and were establishing themselves as the ancestors of the Bantu-speaking peoples who today inhabit all of Africa south of the equator.

The peoples of western Africa reached the southern part of what is now the Republic of South Africa as recently as the fifteenth century. The southerly movement of these peoples, into lands formerly inhabited by a different, Khoisan population, took place partly by intermarriage with the indigenous peoples and partly by conquest. When Europeans settled at the Cape of Good Hope in the middle of the seventeenth century, the southerly African migration had completely absorbed or exterminated the Khoisan peoples everywhere except in what is now the Cape Province of South Africa and in parts of modern Botswana and Namibia. The so-called Hottentots of the area and the Bantu-speaking peoples from the north had been in contact—sometimes hostile and sometimes peaceful—for several centuries by the time the European settlers entered the scene.

Since the Saharan period, eight thousand or more years ago, Africans have been moving, and changing, almost up to the present. It was not until European colonial control was established that the various African peoples were fixed—perhaps for only a moment in their history—in given areas. Consequently, the popular Western stereotype of Africa as a "sleeping giant" is not wholly accurate. The movements of Africa's peoples, and of African ideas and cultures, are a dynamic process that stretches over thousands of years, up to the colonial era. It was only during the brief colonial period that Africa was temporarily dormant.

The approximately 400 million residents of the continent of Africa represent many different racial blends. The term "race" is more often confusing than it is helpful. Scientists may use the word "race" as a convenient way to describe a group of individuals, human or animal, that share certain common characteristics. For example, if a group of people all have blond hair, blue eyes, light skin, and long legs, a scientist might call them a race, in order to distinguish them from another group of people who all have black hair, brown eyes, dark skin, and short legs. But the less neatly each individual fits into one of these "races," the less the term means. Of these two hypothetical racial groupings, which one suits individuals who have blond hair, brown eyes, yellow skin, and medium-length legs? Or individuals who have black hair, blue eyes, dark skin, and long legs?

When the indigenous peoples of Africa first came into contact with modern Europe, they were living in a variety of social groupings. In popular usage these social groupings are usually referred to as "tribes." In actual fact, however, the term "tribe" is as inadequate as the term "race" in describing the peoples of Africa.

The groupings in which Africans live range from tiny bands of a few dozen Khoisan to great cities of hundreds of thousands of Yorubas. The Ibo "tribe" of western Africa numbers twelve million people, who live in an extensive area. But the Hadzapi "tribe" of Tanzania numbers fewer than two thousand people, who inhabit a very small area. To describe Africa, it is preferable to avoid the term "tribe" and to use the more accurate (though less concise) term "ethnic group." An

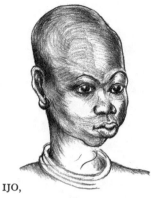

IJO,
SOUTHEASTERN NIGERIA

FULANI,
NORTHERN NIGERIA

ZULU,
SOUTHERN AFRICA

SUDANESE,
EASTERN SUDAN

PEUL,
LAKE CHAD REGION

"ethnic group" means a people who speak the same language, share a common culture, and recognize a common heritage.

There are hundreds of ethnic groups on the continent of Africa. Each of these ethnic groups speaks its own identifiable language—although in some cases the languages are closely related. Many centuries ago the African individual generally spoke only one language. Perhaps, if one group was in close contact with a neighboring group, its members spoke one other language as well. Where large states conquered surrounding peoples, the language of the conquering state became the main language of commerce.

But with the colonial conquest, European languages were superimposed on local languages. The result is that modern Africans often speak their own ethnic language, the European language used in their area, and perhaps one or more of the other African languages. Most modern African nations have retained the language of their former colonial rulers as the official state language. It is in these official languages that Africans of different ethnic groups communicate with each other today.

Keeping in mind these general, cautionary remarks about races, tribes, ethnic groups, and languages, let us take a broad look at the peoples of Africa—their physical characteristics, languages, social groupings, and modern nations. In order to simplify this broad survey, we shall divide Africa into seven large regions: North Africa, West Africa, Central Africa, Southern Africa, East Africa, Madagascar and the Mascarenes, and Northeast Africa.

North Africa includes the modern states of Algeria, Libya, Mauritania, Morocco, Tunisia, and Egypt. All

these states are independent except for a few small enclaves, such as Ceuta, Melilla, and Ifni, which are under Spanish control. All the North African countries border the Sahara Desert, and all border the Mediterranean Sea—except for Mauritania and part of Morocco, which are on the Atlantic Ocean coast.

The predominant physical type of the North African peoples is termed "Mediterranean Caucasoid," with a mixture of Negroid in some areas. In general the North Africans may be described as being of short-to-medium stature with tan or swarthy complexions, straight or curly dark hair, brown or black eyes, thin sharp noses, and thin lips. But there are some genuine North Africans who have quite fair skin; some who have black skin;

some who have tightly curled hair; some who have blue or green eyes; some who have light brown or blondish hair; and some who are quite tall.

For thousands of years North Africa has been a meeting ground for Berbers and Negroes of Africa, Europeans from the Mediterranean area, and Arabs from the Middle East. Each of these peoples has left traces in the physical appearance of the North Africans, with the traits of the Berbers and Arabs being most pronounced.

In language, the Arabs have had the most lasting impact. Although Arabic was brought to North Africa as recently as the seventh and eighth centuries, it has become the native language of the great majority of North Africans. Some North African peoples still use older Berber languages at home, but they are equally fluent in Arabic.

As a consequence of the colonial era, French has become the official language of Algeria, Mauritania, Morocco, and Tunisia. Italian is still widely used in Libya, which was under Italian rule; and Spanish is spoken in the former Spanish Sahara, now divided between Mauritania and Morocco. In Egypt both English and French are spoken by most educated Egyptians, but Arabic is the sole official language.

All the North African peoples have long been accustomed to participation in the processes of a large political state. But in most of these nations there are still strong ethnic groups whose people pay allegiance to their own kings, princes, sheiks, beys, or chiefs as well as to the national king or president. These peoples have been conquered many times by Phoenicians, Greeks, Romans, Arabs, and European colonial powers; yet some local loyalties and traditions have survived. However, Arab customs and speech have made a permanent

MAJOR LANGUAGE GROUPS

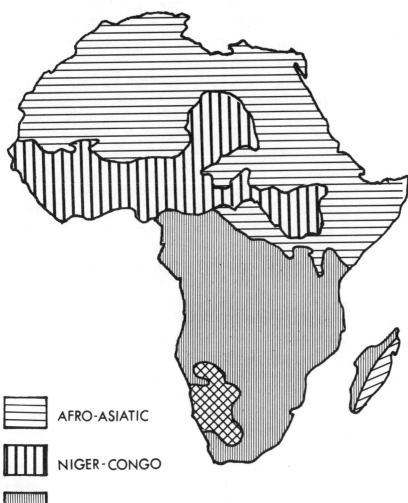

 AFRO-ASIATIC

NIGER-CONGO

NIGER-CONGO: BANTU

KHOISAN

HOVA

impression, and serve to bind the ethnic groups together into large states.

For thousands of years the coastal North Africans
have been a farming people and have traditionally lived
in small towns or villages. In the Sahara Desert the
North Africans have either settled in the fertile oases or
led a nomadic life, herding camels, goats, and sheep.
There have been large towns and cities for centuries in
North Africa; but they have been established by foreign
conquerors, gradually attracting North African residents from the countryside over a long period of
growth.

Today North Africa boasts many large, modern cities, such as Casablanca and Rabat in Morocco, Tunis in
Tunisia, Algiers and Constantine in Algeria, and Cairo
in Egypt. In these cities live millions of North Africans,
who are educated and urbanized, as well as large
groups of French, Spanish, Italian, and other foreign
peoples.

Politically Morocco is a monarchy, but all the other
North African countries are republics. Algeria, Egypt,
and Libya are ruled by military leaders whose factions
seized power by force. None, however, are considered
dictatorships. The former Spanish Sahara was occupied
by Mauritania and Morocco in 1975 and has since been
divided between these two nations, despite Algerian
claims to part of the territory.

All the North African states class themselves as African countries and play a full role in intra-African affairs
such as the Organization for African Unity. But these
countries play a role in Middle Eastern affairs as well,
because of their linguistic, cultural, and historical ties
with the Arab world.

West Africa is the largest and most populous region
of Africa, with fourteen independent states and a popu-

lation of about 120 million people. Nine West African countries were French colonies: Benin, Guinea, Ivory Coast, Mali, Mauritania, Niger, Senegal, Togo, and Upper Volta. Four were under British control: Gambia, Ghana, Nigeria, and Sierra Leone. Guinea-Bissau was long under Portuguese rule. And one, Liberia, has the longest history of uninterrupted independence (since 1847) of any nation in Africa—and is indeed one of the oldest republics in the world.

The West African peoples are generally Negroid in their physical characteristics. They are predominantly medium-to-dark brown in skin color, with thick, tightly curled hair; brown eyes; broad noses; and fleshy lips. As always, however, there are exceptions. There are some West Africans with dark skin and straight black hair; others with hazel or green eyes; and still others with thin lips and sharp noses. Mixture with Berbers and Arabs in the central and northern parts of West Africa and with Europeans in the coastal areas has resulted in a small number of individuals who resemble "typical" North Africans more than "typical" West Africans.

A great variety of native languages are spoken in

West Africa, most of which belong to the large Niger-Congo linguistic family. Many of these languages are tonal in quality; that is, the meanings of different words depend in part on the musical pitch, or tone, at which the word or syllable is spoken. Since this tonal quality can be partially duplicated by certain resonant drums, there is a tradition in West Africa of using the "talking" drum for communication over long distances. A few of the more important West African languages are Bambara, Ewe, Fulani, Hausa, Kru, Ibo, Malinke, Mende, Twi, Yoruba, and Wolof.

SLIT DRUM, ZAIRE

As a consequence of the British and French colonial domination of West African territory, English and French remain the official languages. Gambia, Ghana, Nigeria, Sierra Leone, and Liberia use English, while French is used in all the other states of West Africa, except Guinea-Bissau, which uses Portuguese.

There are many ethnic groups in West Africa, several of them numbering over ten million people. Among the largest ethnic groups are the Ibo and Yoruba peoples of Nigeria; the Hausa people of Niger and Nigeria; the Ashanti and Fanti of Ghana; the Ewe of Ghana and Togo; the Mende of Guinea and Sierra Leone; the Wolof of Guinea and Senegal; the Bambara of Mali and surrounding countries; and the Fulani, who live in a number of countries in interior West Africa.

The West African peoples tend to be educationally and culturally advanced compared with those of other African regions. The peoples of the coastal regions have long been in communication with Europe, and

A WEST AFRICAN ASHANTI KING

schools were established there quite early. But long before direct contact with Europe, West Africa produced wealthy and powerful states with their own distinctive civilizations. West Africans often wear colorful dress and engage in much pageantry—drumming and dancing ceremonies, great religious festivals, parades, elaborate coronation ceremonies, and outdoor plays. A visit to a market in West Africa is an unforgettable experience. Hundreds of stalls and booths brim with food and goods; throngs of gaily dressed, talkative people shop; there is an exciting confusion of sounds, sights, and smells.

West Africa has traditionally been a region of towns and cities. Trading centers established at key transportation points have in some cases grown into large cities, with populations in excess of 100,000. Several cities that were major centers hundreds of years ago are still in existence: Kano, Katsina, Sokoto, Benin, and Ibadan in Nigeria; Kumasi in Ghana; Gao and Timbuktu in Mali. Most West African cities are surrounded by a sizable hinterland of farms and villages.

Each city in West Africa is populated largely by members of a single ethnic group, such as the Bini people in Benin, the Yoruba in Ibadan, the Hausa in Kano, and the Ashanti in Kumasi. But each city also has a minority of settlers from other groups. They come—sometimes great distances—to trade or to perform specialized work, such as goldsmithing, fishing, clerical work, or weaving. This gives the cities a very cosmopolitan quality.

YORUBA
WOMAN

Many centuries ago the peoples of the interior of West Africa were prosperous and powerful, while those in the coastal rain-forest belt were weaker and less prosperous. In modern times this balance has been reversed, because the coastal peoples have traded with

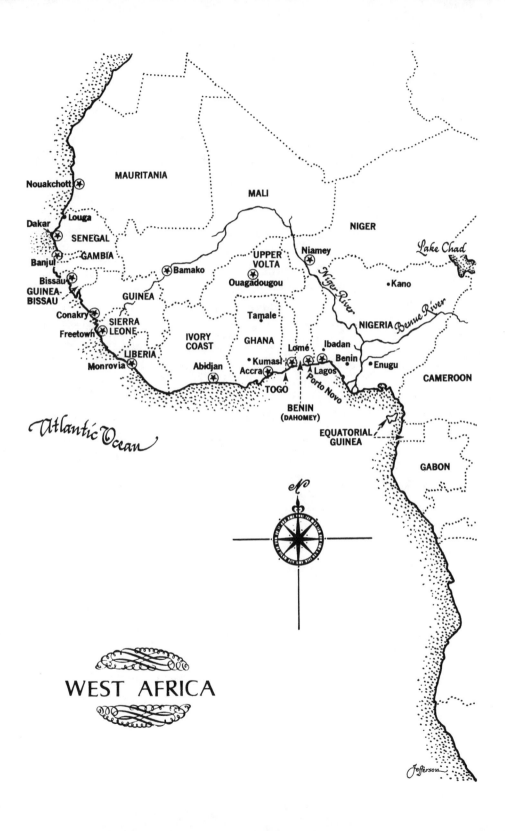

Nouakchott

MAURITANIA

MALI

NIGER

Lake Chad

Louga

Dakar

SENEGAL

Niamey

Niger River

Banjul

GAMBIA

Bamako

UPPER
VOLTA

Bissau

Ouagadougou

Kano

GUINEA-
BISSAU

GUINEA

Benue River

Conakry

SIERRA
LEONE

Tamale

NIGERIA

Freetown

IVORY
COAST

GHANA

Ibadan

Liberia

Lomé

Benin

LIBERIA

Kumasi

Enugu

Monrovia

Abidjan

Accra

Lagos

CAMEROON

TOGO

Porto Novo

BENIN
(DAHOMEY)

Atlantic Ocean

EQUATORIAL
GUINEA

GABON

N

WEST AFRICA

Jefferson

Europe and had greater access to modern education, while their mineral, forest, and crop resources became more fully developed.

Ghana, Ivory Coast, and Nigeria in particular have prospered—especially their southern regions near the coast.

Ghana was already developing prior to independence in 1957, and its rate of development has increased since. More than 50 percent of its people are literate, and it has thousands of educated citizens with experience in government administration, business, and the professions. The Fanti and Ga peoples along Ghana's coast have conducted international trade for over four centuries, while the Ashanti of the central part of the country developed a rich and powerful empire of their own. In modern Ghana these peoples form the nucleus of a population noted for its energy and progressive ambitions.

Ivory Coast, Ghana's neighbor to the west, is in many respects similar to Ghana, although French is spoken there. In recent years its people have made great strides in mining, agriculture, and industry; and its capital city, Abidjan, has become one of the most important in West Africa as a port and as a financial and commercial center.

Nigeria is the most populous country in Africa, and potentially the continent's most powerful nation. When it became independent in 1960, Nigeria was a federation of three very different parts: the Northern Region, dominated by the Hausa people; the Western Region, dominated by the Yoruba people; and the Eastern Region, dominated by the Ibo people. United by federation, these regions began to develop rapidly, and Nigeria's great size and potential wealth attracted world attention.

In 1966, however, the Nigerian army seized power, and most of the political leaders were killed. Following another coup by a different army faction later the same year, the Eastern Region began to pull away from the federation, seceding in 1967 as the independent state of Biafra. Civil war ensued, and Nigeria's exemplary development was arrested. The federation forces eventually prevailed, after one of the bloodiest civil wars in modern history, but the toll, in money, human lives, and national development, was great.

After the war's end, oil production resumed and increased steadily, until today Nigeria is one of the world's major oil producers. Oil revenues, now very great, are being used to speed up development in all parts of this large, populous nation.

While the coastal nations have tended to prosper, the West African interior nations of Mali, Niger, and Upper Volta are confronted with serious obstacles to development. All three countries are sparsely populated, with large areas of poor soil and low rainfall. They have not had the direct contact with the rest of the world that was of benefit to the coastal peoples. And, because modern education reached them only in the twentieth century, relatively few of their citizens are literate.

World attention has focused on these countries since the terrible drought that reached its peak in 1973. Much of their territory lies in the Sahel region, which borders the Sahara Desert and in the best of years has only light rainfall. Rains were unusually poor from 1967 to 1973, causing the deaths of thousands of people and millions of livestock in these three countries and in other interior parts of West Africa. After 1974 increased rain brought better conditions, but many of the rural people still suffer from poverty and malnutrition.

Liberia and Sierra Leone, on the western Atlantic

coast, have many similarities: they are small in area and population, their interiors were isolated until recent years, and they were both founded by freed slaves. Both countries have had rapid economic development since World War II, and both have great mineral wealth.

Benin, Guinea, Mauritania, Senegal, and Togo, the remaining nations of West Africa's coast, were all once part of French West Africa, administered from the city of Dakar, Senegal. But they are very different from one another and have followed separate courses of development since achieving their independence.

Historically, Benin and Togo are closely related to their neighbors, Ghana and Nigeria. They are very small countries, and neither has discovered significant mineral wealth. Their coastal peoples are well educated and progressive, but both countries are so poor that many of their educated citizens move to other West African countries to work.

Guinea, largely because of its fierce determination to break away from France in 1958, has been isolated from its French-speaking neighbors since independence. Starting with little money, industry, or skilled manpower, it signed aid treaties with the Soviet Union, the United States, and other countries. Still a comparatively poor country, it has discovered mineral reserves and is beginning to progress.

Senegal, which was ruled by France for over two hundred years, is an economically poor country, but it has a well-educated population and close cultural ties with France. Its capital, Dakar, is one of the most modern and sophisticated cities in Africa, but the Senegalese interior is still underdeveloped.

Mauritania, most of which lies in the Sahara Desert, is a unique blend of West Africa and North Africa. Among its population are both Negroid peoples and

Caucasoid Berbers; but all are Moslem and are Arabic-speaking. Although the people are proud and have a rich history, the land is very poor and undeveloped.

Gambia is the smallest country in West Africa. It consists of a narrow strip of territory on both sides of the Gambia River, which reaches three hundred miles from the Atlantic Ocean into the interior of Senegal. Senegal surrounds Gambia on three sides. The English-speaking Gambians are closely related to the French-speaking Senegalese, but they have developed their own national outlook, based on their long contact with the British.

The newly independent state of Guinea-Bissau, formerly Portuguese Guinea, is also in West Africa. After many years of bitter armed struggle by its people, it gained independence from Portugal in 1974. A small, tropical land, it is just beginning to develop itself after a long period of stagnation.

The modern states of West Africa adopted republican forms of government when they achieved independence from colonial rule. Thus each established a president or prime minister, and an elected parliament or legislative assembly. But since independence many of these nations have experienced internal restiveness, and military coups have taken place in Benin, Ghana, Nigeria, Sierra Leone, Togo, and Upper Volta. In each of these countries a ruling council or junta of army officers seized power and dismissed the parliament or assembly, intending to rule until it could restore financial stability and impartial governmental administration.

To the southeast of West Africa lies the region known as Central Africa, comprising the countries of Cameroon, the Central African Empire, Chad, Congo (Brazzaville), Zaire, and Gabon. They all use French as their official language, although Cameroon uses English as well in its western region. All the Central African countries were formerly French colonies except for West Cameroon, which was British, and Zaire, which was Belgian. Zaire, was originally called the Belgian Congo, then Congo (Kinshasa), until it adopted the African name of Zaire in 1970.

The peoples of Central Africa are physically much like the West Africans. There is somewhat less mixture with Arab, Berber, and European stock, except in small parts of Zaire, where the Portuguese have long maintained contact with the Bakongo people. Several groups of Twa peoples, or "Pygmies," live in Central Africa. They are racially distinct, with lighter skin color, diminutive stature, and such other characteristics as different concentrations of blood types.

Most of the native languages spoken in Central Africa are of the great Niger-Congo linguistic family, with the majority belonging to the widespread Bantu subfamily. Among the more important languages are Bamileke, Douala, Fang, Kikongo, Lingala, and Umbundu. Arabic is spoken in parts of the Central African Empire and in Chad, but it is unimportant in most of Central Africa.

The peoples of Central Africa have historically been village dwellers; consequently few large towns or cities have developed there. In general their ethnic groups are spread loosely over an area ruled by a local village or clan chief. But there are important exceptions where ancient kings united many villages and chiefdoms into well-organized states, as in the Baluba, Balunda, and Bakongo areas of modern Zaire and northern Angola.

As elsewhere, the colonial era brought a very different political organization to Central Africa. Prior to independence the Central African Empire, Chad, Congo (Brazzaville), and Gabon were all part of one

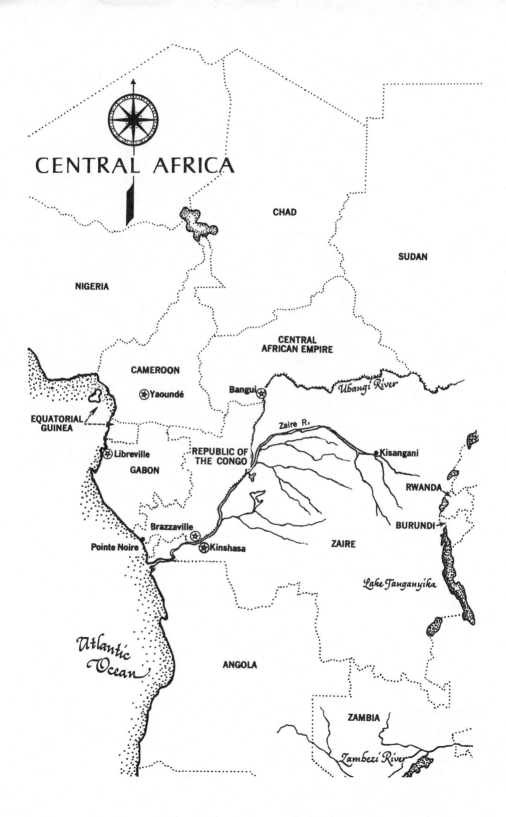

CENTRAL AFRICA

CHAD

SUDAN

NIGERIA

CENTRAL
AFRICAN EMPIRE

CAMEROON

⊕ Yaoundé

Bangui ⊕

Ubangi River

EQUATORIAL
GUINEA

Zaire R.

Kisangani

⊕ Libreville

REPUBLIC OF
THE CONGO

GABON

RWANDA

BURUNDI

Brazzaville ⊕

Pointe Noire

⊛ Kinshasa

ZAIRE

Lake Tanganyika

Atlantic
Ocean

ANGOLA

ZAMBIA

Zambezi River

huge territory—French Equatorial Africa, the capital of which was Brazzaville, on the Zaire (Congo) River.

Cameroon is a unique federal state. It was created when part of the former British Cameroons, which had been administered jointly with Nigeria, voted to unite with the French territory of Cameroon to form a single nation, the Federal Republic of Cameroon.

The most notable nation in Central Africa is Zaire. It is a vast land that radiates outward from the Zaire basin rain forest. In the late nineteenth century it was investigated by Henry Morton Stanley, the famous American journalist turned explorer, after his meeting with Doctor Livingstone in the interior of Tanganyika. Stanley's several expeditions in the Congo were carried out under the sponsorship of Leopold II, king of the Belgians, who in 1884 established personal claim to the Congo and thereby helped to precipitate the European rush to divide up Africa.

In this colonial partitioning, the French, pushing inland from the Gabon coast, laid claim to that portion of the Congo north and west of the Congo River. The Portuguese had already claimed much of the territory south and east of the river, so that King Leopold eventually settled for a narrow corridor to the sea sandwiched between the French and the Portuguese territory. The result was two Congo states—one French and one Belgian. And to confuse matters further, the indigenous Bakongo people were divided among the French Congo, the Belgian Congo, and Angola, which was under the Portuguese.

But King Leopold's Congo claim, based on Stanley's explorations and treaties with African kings, extended up the Congo River into the interior to cover a vast area that today is the third largest country in Africa. Rich in resources, the Congo was developed under King Leopold and later Belgian administrations into one of the richest mining and industrial states in Africa. Leopold's ruthless methods of development unfortunately included forced labor, the use of troops to murder recalcitrant peoples, and a complete denial of legal and democratic rights to the Congolese. Horrified world opinion eventually resulted in transfer of the Congo's administration to the Belgian parliament and in the elimination of some of the worst abuses.

The heritage of Belgian rule, however, was that the Congo developed economically while its people gained little higher education or experience in modern government. When independence came in 1960, the Congolese had had no previous opportunity to govern their large and diverse nation. The result was serious internal strife and secessionist movements that left little chance for the African leaders to carry on the country's economic development.

Today Zaire is firmly ruled by President Mobutu Sese Seko, a former army officer. He has brought all parts of the country under the control of the central government and has launched a development plan, but has to use military force and outside assistance in suppressing revolts by various groups.

Gabon, a nation little known to Americans except as the location of Albert Schweitzer's hospital, is one of the wealthier countries in Africa. It produces a number of wood products, manganese, cocoa, peanuts, and bananas. Gabon has extensive iron deposits as well as promising possibilities for production of oil and natural gas.

The Central African Empire and Chad are isolated and underdeveloped. They lie many hundreds of miles from ocean port facilities and have poor internal transportation routes. Both have large areas of poor soil and low rainfall; Chad is nearly half desert. Both countries are in the tsetse-fly zone.

Equatorial Guinea, formerly the colony of Spanish Guinea, became independent in 1968.

The nations of Central Africa have experienced much governmental instability in the years since independence. The Central African Empire, Congo, and Zaire have had military coups, and Gabon has had to call on French troops to protect its government. Zaire has seen several drastic changes in its government, and even civil war, although it has become more stable since General Mobutu Sese Seko became President in 1966. For a few years after independence, Cameroon experienced great unrest in the former French section, with outbreaks of guerrilla fighting; but it has been at peace since 1962.

A small portion of Central Africa is still under European rule: Portugal controls two small islands off the coast of Cameroon—São Tomé and Principe.

The region of Southern Africa stretches from Angola on the Atlantic Ocean south to the Republic of South Africa, and also includes Botswana (formerly Bechuanaland), Lesotho (formerly Basutoland), Malawi (formerly Nyasaland), Mozambique, Namibia (South-West Africa), Swaziland, Zambia (formerly Northern Rhodesia), and Zimbabwe (the nationalist name for Rhodesia).

Until 1966 the Republic of South Africa was the only independent nation in Southern Africa, but in that year Botswana and Lesotho gained their independence. Swaziland followed in 1968, and Angola and Mozambique, after years of armed struggle against the Portuguese, were freed in 1975. Zimbabwe is wracked by a war for liberation against the ruling white-settler minority, and both African nationalists and the United Nations are trying to free Namibia from South African

Luanda

Lobito

ANGOLA

ZAMBIA

Lusaka

Zambezi River

Kariba Dam

MALAWI

Lilongwe

Salisbury

ZIMBABWE
(RHODESIA)

• Bulawayo

NAMIBIA
(S. W. AFRICA)

MOZAMBIQUE

Windhoek

BOTSWANA

Kalahari Desert

Limpopo River

Gaberones

Orange River

Pretoria

Johannesburg

Mbabane

Maputo

SWAZILAND

Kimberley

LESOTHO

Maseru

Durban

Atlantic
Ocean

SOUTH AFRICA

Indian Ocean

Capetown

N

Jefferson

SOUTHERN AFRICA

control. Soon the Republic of South Africa will be the only country in the region that is not ruled by Africans.

English is the official language in Botswana, Lesotho, Malawi, Zimbabwe, Swaziland, and Zambia. Namibia and the Republic of South Africa use both English and Afrikaans, a language related to Dutch. Angola and Mozambique use Portuguese.

Many races have settled in Southern Africa. Originally it was populated by a distinct race—the Khoisan peoples. These peoples, known to Europeans as Bushmen and Hottentots, were once the indigenous population of nearly half the African continent, but gradually were supplanted by Negroid peoples, except in the very tip of the continent. Of small stature, they had yellowish skin, heavy ridges above their eyes, and tightly curled hair. Most were hunters of game and gatherers of wild roots and berries, although the so-called Hottentots had, by about A.D. 1000, begun to depend on herding cattle and goats for a living.

By A.D. 200 Negroid, Bantu-speaking peoples began to settle the region, and by 1500 they had pushed south to within a few hundred miles of the Cape of Good Hope. During the seventeenth century Dutch settlers colonized the Cape area; these were later joined by French, German, and British immigrants. For a time slaves from Malaysia and West Africa were imported into South Africa, later followed by Indian laborers. Portuguese settlers occupied parts of Angola and Mozambique from the early sixteenth century.

The result of these migrations to the region is a population that includes more than 35,000,000 Negroid Africans, 5,000,000 Europeans, 2,000,000 mixed people called "Coloureds," 750,000 Indians, and small numbers of remaining Khoisan peoples.

NDEBELE GIRL

Almost all the indigenous Africans of the Southern

Africa region speak languages belonging to the Bantu subfamily: Sesotho, Zulu, Xhosa, Sechuana, Mashona, Ovambo, Sindebele, Bemba, and others. The few surviving groups of Khoisan speak languages of the Khoisan family, which uses a number of clicks and guttural sounds.

Prior to the twentieth century almost all the indigenous Southern African people were both grain farmers and cattle herders. They settled in villages and small towns but developed no cities. Many were seminomadic, moving every few years to find better grazing lands for their cattle or to allow their farm soil to regain its fertility. Several groups became widely known for their superior military organization, the most famous being the Zulu people under King Shaka. These warlike people controlled large territories, conquering neighboring groups and absorbing them into an empire.

The whole region of Southern Africa in modern times is beset by racial tensions, caused by the great inequality in wealth and power between the white and the African populations. In Namibia, South Africa, and Zimbabwe, white minorities have maintained tight control over much larger black majorities, allowing them no political rights and relegating them to the poorest lands and the lower-paid jobs.

The Republic of South Africa is the wealthiest and best-developed country in Africa, and its white population enjoys one of the highest standards of living in the world. It has great mineral and agricultural wealth, and is heavily industrialized. But in building and maintaining the wealth of its white population, it has developed increasingly into a totalitarian state. Its government imprisons people who oppose it, without trial or legal charges, and forbids political activity of any kind among the black population. Since 1976 major riots and unrest have resulted from black protests against this oppression.

The South African government, claiming that it is giving some of its African peoples freedom, has created the new states of the Transkei and Baphutatswana, which are not recognized by any country in the world. These small, impoverished territories are viewed by most Africans as puppet states with no real freedom or potentiality for development.

Botswana, Lesotho, and Swaziland are all small African nations, poor and struggling to develop. Economically they are heavily dependent on the Republic of South Africa.

The white population of Zimbabwe (Rhodesia) is much smaller than that of the Republic of South Africa, but also rules oppressively over a large African majority. A fierce guerrilla struggle has been going on there for several years, which the African liberation forces are expected to win eventually.

Angola and Mozambique won independence in 1974, after long and bitter warfare against the Portuguese. Mozambique is beginning slowly to develop under the leadership of a political party called FRELIMO, but Angola has been torn by internal struggles since independence. Its central government is led by the Popular Movement for the Liberation of Angola (MPLA).

Namibia was a German colony until World War I, when the Republic (then Union) of South Africa defeated its German defenders. First declared a League of Nations mandate, administered by South Africa, South-West Africa later became a trust territory when the United Nations was created. South Africa has tried to maintain tight control over the country, but the United Nations is exerting ever stronger pressures to force South Africa to relinquish control and allow the African

ANGOLAN MAN

people to form an independent Namibia.

Malawi is a small country whose economy is heavily dependent on the Republic of South Africa. It has little mineral wealth and is mainly rural. Zambia, on the other hand, has major copper mines, which it has managed to develop itself without falling under strong South Africa influence. It maintains close political and communication links with Tanzania, to its north.

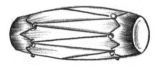

Off the Indian Ocean coast of Africa, opposite Mozambique, lies the large island of Madagascar; to the north are the smaller islands of Mauritius and Reunion (the Mascarenes) and groups of still smaller islands called the Comoros and the Seychelles. All are considered part of Africa, despite their distance from the continent.

Madagascar is now the independent Malagasy Republic, and both Mauritius and the Seychelles are independent nations. France controls the Comoros and Reunion. All these islands have been under French rule at one time or another, and they were settled by the French as well as by Africans, Indians, and Polynesians. French is widely spoken, even in Mauritius and the Seychelles, where English is the official language. The native Malagasy language is related to Malay, but it includes many Arabic and Bantu words. Many of the African settlers of Madagascar speak Bantu languages, but most of them also use Malagasy.

One of the largest regions on the African continent is East Africa, consisting of Burundi, Kenya, Rwanda, Tanzania, and Uganda. The peoples of East Africa are of several racial backgrounds, but the majority are Bantu-speaking Negroes. There are smaller groups of Arabs; Asians, from India and Pakistan; and Europeans, largely from Britain.

English is the official language of Kenya, Tanzania, and Uganda. French is used in Burundi and Rwanda. Most of the native languages in the region are of the Bantu subfamily, but a minority of the African groups speak Nilotic languages. Among the more important languages of East Africa are Swahili, Kikuyu, Luo, Luganda, Kirundi, Kinyarwanda, and Kikamba. Along the coast of East Africa are settlements of Arabs, who speak Arabic as well as Swahili. Swahili, together with English, is an official national language in Tanzania; it is also widely used in other parts of East Africa.

Prior to World War I, Germany administered a large area known as German East Africa. But following the war, Britain assumed control of the countries of Tanganyika and Zanzibar. These later gained independence and united, in 1965, to form the United Republic of Tanzania. After World War I, Belgium assumed control of the area known as Ruanda-Urundi. In 1962 this territory split into independent Rwanda and Burundi.

Britain has long been a major influence in East Africa, administering Kenya and Uganda before it acquired Tanganyika and Zanzibar.

Although East Africa is a populous region, with roughly 50 million people, it is so large in area that it is sparsely settled, except in a few areas of high soil fertility. The more densely populated parts include Burundi and Rwanda, the highlands of Kenya, and the parts of Kenya, Tanzania, and Uganda that border on Lake Victoria. Until modern times most of the people of East Africa lived in small villages—though in a few instances these villages grew large enough to be consid-

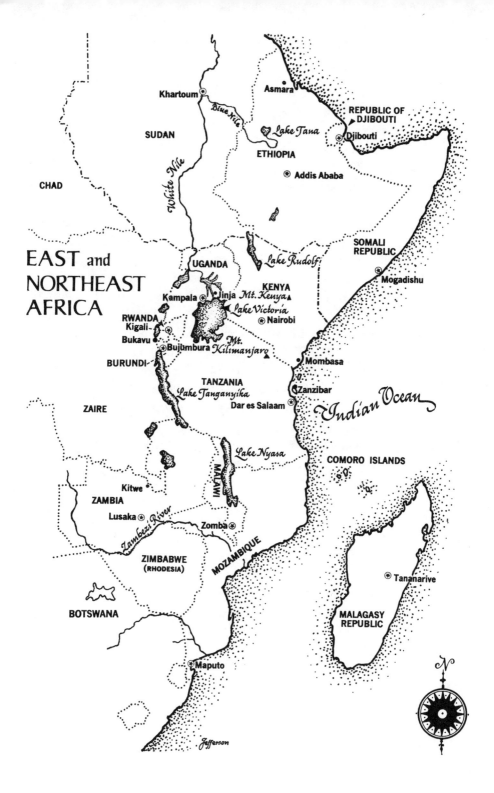

EAST and
NORTHEAST
AFRICA

CHAD

SUDAN

Khartoum

Blue Nile

White Nile

Asmara

REPUBLIC OF
DJIBOUTI

Djibouti

Lake Tana

ETHIOPIA

Addis Ababa

SOMALI
REPUBLIC

Lake Rudolf

Mogadishu

UGANDA

Kampala

Jinja

Mt. Kenya

KENYA

Lake Victoria

Nairobi

RWANDA
Kigali

Bukavu

Bujumbura

Mt. Kilimanjaro

BURUNDI

Mombasa

TANZANIA

Lake Tanganyika

Zanzibar

Dar es Salaam

Indian Ocean

ZAIRE

Lake Nyasa

COMORO ISLANDS

MALAWI

Kitwe

ZAMBIA

Lusaka

Zambezi River

Zomba

MOZAMBIQUE

ZIMBABWE
(RHODESIA)

Tananarive

BOTSWANA

MALAGASY
REPUBLIC

Maputo

Jefferson

ered small cities. Along the coast of East Africa major cities did develop more than a thousand years ago, inhabited by Bantu-speaking Africans and by Arabs from the Red Sea and Persian Gulf lands.

The climate and soils of the highlands of Kenya and Tanzania have proved attractive for settlers from Europe. By 1960 there were nearly 100,000 white settlers in these areas. Since these countries have become independent, some of the whites have emigrated to the Republic of South Africa, Canada, and New Zealand; but others remain as citizens of the new nations.

Laborers from India and Pakistan were brought to East Africa when the railroads were built, and most settled in the area permanently. Today they number about 300,000, over half of whom have taken citizenship in the new nations. In 1972 Uganda expelled most of its Asians, including many who had become citizens. Although many of the Asians are employed as unskilled or semiskilled laborers, a large number have opened businesses or have become teachers, doctors, lawyers, architects, and engineers.

East Africa has gained considerable world attention. It has the largest herds of wild game on earth, as well as many other attractions of interest to foreign tourists. Its mines, cash crops, and industries have attracted foreign investors. And the unique multiracial character of its new nations, with often several racial elements attempting to live harmoniously together, has interested many foreign observers.

But the features that have attracted foreign attention have also increased the gap between the living standards in East Africa's cities and its rural areas. The cities are populated by wealthy European and Asian businessmen and professional people and by African government leaders and civil servants, all enjoying a very high standard of living. East Africa's cities are modern and prosperous, surrounded by lovely residential areas. The rural areas, on the other hand, are populated by African peasants who live humbly, barely touched by the wealth and modernity of the cities. Rural development, to improve this situation is a high priority for East African governments.

Economically the nations of East Africa are not highly developed. Kenya has a variety of small industries and also exports coffee, tea, sisal, and other agricultural and mineral products. Uganda produces tea, sugar, and coffee; has exploited some of its mineral reserves, such as copper, cobalt, and phosphates; and built up its industries rapidly until about 1972, when the expulsion of Asians and the capricious policies of dictator Idi Amin produced a serious decline. Tanzania, a major producer of sisal and diamonds, also exports gold, coffee, pyrethrum, cashews, cloves, and a number of other mineral and agricultural commodities. It, too, is beginning to develop its manufacturing.

Like other parts of Africa, the nations of East Africa have experienced a certain amount of unrest since achieving independence. Burundi has had military coups with several bloody purges of many thousands of people. Before Tanzania was formed, Tanganyika's troops mutinied and were subdued by British troops, and Zanzibar had a major revolution. Both Rwanda and Uganda have had serious civil disturbances, and thousands of people were murdered in Uganda.

By 1968 most East African nations had become more stable, and all except Burundi and Uganda were governed by democratically elected governments. But many leaders in the area expect future unrest because

of the frustrations of the peasants and the unemployed, even though strong efforts are being made to achieve progress and stability.

North of East Africa is the region of Northeast Africa, often called "the Horn" because of the shape of its eastern tip. The tiny Republic of Djibouti (formerly French Somaliland), Ethiopia, Somalia (Somali Republic), and Sudan make up the region. Both Ethiopia and Somalia have in recent years maintained ties with the nations of East Africa, while Sudan has identified partially with North Africa. But the three countries have many racial and historical similarities. The region has been of special interest to Europeans because it was strongly influenced by the ancient Egyptian, Greek, Roman, and Arab civilizations, which also contributed to the development of what is now modern Europe.

The peoples of Northeast Africa range from definitely Negroid in type to partly Caucasoid. The "typical" African of the region is almost impossible to define, but most frequently found are very light to tan skins, curly hair, sharp noses, and relatively thin lips. In build, the population tends to be of medium height or tall, and slim rather than heavy. In the southern part of Sudan most of the people are Negroid in type and—like the closely related Nilotic people of East Africa—tend to be tall and slim.

Most people of Northeast Africa speak languages of the Afro-Asian family. This large language family includes many African languages, such as Amharic and Somali, as well as Asian languages, such as Arabic and Hebrew. The Nilotic peoples of southern Sudan speak languages of the Sudanic family. Most Somalis and northern Sudanese, and some Ethiopians, are Moslem in religion, and speak Arabic. This was for many centuries an area of Arab conquest and development.

Although there are many Ethiopians who are Moslem, Ethiopia has been a stronghold of Christianity since the fourth century. The ruling Amhara people have lived on the high mountains and plateaus for many centuries and have developed a "mountain fastness" personality. They have defended their Coptic Christian religion and way of life against the surrounding Moslems and against early Portuguese missionaries who sought to unite them with Roman Catholicism.

In Sudan and Ethiopia, agriculture has been the means of subsistence for thousands of years. Most of the people live on farmlands and in villages, but there have long been large towns and cities. In both countries, the cities have played an influential role, uniting the agricultural areas around them into city-states.

Most Somalis, and some Ethiopians and Sudanese, have depended on cattle herding as a way of life, and there are many nomadic peoples in the region.

Along the coasts of Ethiopia and Somalia are settlements of fishing and seafaring peoples. Like the coastal peoples of East Africa, they have long traded the gold, ivory, skins, and spices of Africa for the pottery, silks, and manufactured goods of Arabia and India.

Throughout Northeast Africa, societies with strong governments have traditionally existed. Powerful kings or emperors ruled their own peoples and conquered others to form states or empires.

The modern nations of Northeast Africa have an intertwined history, but there is still recurrent tension between them. They dispute territory as they have done for centuries. Ethiopia and Somalia have struggled militarily over Djibouti and the Ogaden, an area administered by Ethiopia but inhabited by nomadic Somali herdsmen.

Sudan is the most highly developed of the three na-

HAILE SELASSIE
OF ETHIOPIA

tions, educationally and economically; but Ethiopia is making strides, especially in farming. Ethiopia is one of the most fertile areas in Africa. Although it exports little except coffee, its land supports over 25 million people —a fairly dense population. Somalia is mainly semiarid herding country, but bananas, grown in moist areas near the coast, are its chief export.

Ethiopia has not developed a European system of government, education, and law, as colonial territories tended to do. It has its own culture and institutions. English is fairly widely spoken in the country and is used as a medium of instruction in most Ethiopian high schools.

Politically Ethiopia was a monarchy until Emperor Haile Selassie was deposed in 1974. It is now ruled by a military group, which is fighting a civil war against secessionists in the northern coastal province of Eritrea.

Sudan, under British rule before independence in 1956, adopted English as an official language along with Arabic. It uses a British system of education and retains many British institutions.

Before independence part of Somalia was British, and part was Italian. Since becoming independent, Somalia has used Somali and Arabic as official languages; but English is widely spoken by government officials and better-educated people in the north, and Italian by educated people in the south. The people of Djibouti use French and Arabic.

The Sudanese government was seized by its army in 1958, and Sudan has been governed since that time by a small group of military officers. Somalia, a republic, had its first radical change in government in 1969, when, after its president was assassinated, a military junta seized power.

◀ 4 ▶

The Glory
of Ancient Africa

One of the Western world's most stereotyped ideas about Africa is that it is a continent without a history. Before 1950 most of the great universities of Europe and America taught only the history of the colonial era in Africa, the history of the European settlement of South Africa, or Egyptology as a subject unrelated to any study of the rest of Africa.

This idea has been strongly reinforced by the reports of many modern European and American visitors to Africa. Outside the modern cities built by the colonial rulers, they see that Africans live in villages, till the soil in small plots, herd cattle and goats, or fish for a meager living. It is difficult for most of these visitors to form an impression that is not based on their preconceived ideas of African history, although many Afro-Americans now visit Africa to reestablish their sense of roots.

In its crudest form, this stereotype represents the African as a Stone Age primitive who has lived more or less the same kind of life, without progress, since time immemorial. Africans are looked on as having existed in primitive stagnation until white Europeans came to liberate them from their age-old lethargy.

The facts, which are very different, have come to public attention only in the past few years. Africa has a rich and lively history. Its peoples have long been involved in a great process of movement and development. Entirely African civilizations have flowered, rising to greatness and glory, only to decline in the past few centuries, leaving few traces or memorials. And where evidence and records remained, Europeans often ignored them or stored them away, because they were at variance with the general conception of Africa. The reasons for this are many—not all of them creditable to Europe's explorers, traders, and scholars.

There were available to Europeans in early days a few revealing descriptions of ancient African states and empires, but this information was unnoticed or ignored. The Moorish scholars in Spain and Portugal wrote of ancient Ghana, Mali, Axum, and East Africa, but their works were put aside when the Spanish and Portuguese recaptured their countries. Occasional Portuguese and Dutch visitors to West Africa wrote of the impressive kingdoms they visited; but their reports, too, had little impact.

Most of the Europeans who visited Africa in the fifteenth, sixteenth, and seventeenth centuries were poorly educated ship captains and crewmen, interested only in new sea routes or in profitable trading. When they found evidence of prosperity and civilization in Africa, they often misrepresented the facts in order to discourage their rivals. The Portuguese, who were the earliest Europeans to have extensive commerce with Africa, found a rich trade in gold, ivory, spices, and— somewhat later—slaves. They jealously guarded their knowledge of Africa for fear that the Dutch, British, and French might become competitors (as they soon did).

Africa, particularly after the end of the sixteenth century, was not hospitable to Europeans. They were confined to trading primarily along the coasts and, consequently, had no opportunity to see at first hand the African interior. At that time, prosperity and high development existed there, especially in Mali, Songhay, Kanem-Bornu, and other Sudanic states. These states had no direct access to the coast, but traded through smaller coastal states whose kings thrived as middlemen in the growing trade between interior Africa and the ships of Europe, and maintained their monopoly by restricting the Europeans to the sea.

The commerce between Europe and Africa, originally based on the gold, ivory, spices, and oils of Africa, soon developed the even more lucrative slave trade, which flourished from the middle of the sixteenth century to the early nineteenth. In order to protect their trade from the moral scruples of people in Europe, the slavers developed their own propaganda about Africa. More and more frequently, Africans were represented as savages naturally fit for slavery. And the peoples of Europe and America perhaps wanted to believe this, in order to keep the horrible truth of slavery from themselves.

Thus, what little may have been known originally of the Africa of great states, peaceful peoples, and wise governments was quietly forgotten. By the early nine-

GOLD WEIGHT, BENIN

teenth century Africa had become the Dark Continent. It was regarded, in ignorant awe, as a land of savages, cannibals, superstitious pagans—a land of cruel, warlike black men who were not fully human.

Between 4000 and 1500 B.C., at a time when most of the world was "dark," Africa was the home of the world's greatest civilization: Egypt. The highly advanced Africans living then along the lower Nile were a mighty world power, and they had a written history already many centuries old.

The Egyptians were in close contact with other peoples far up the Nile, in what is now Sudan. These Africans farther south were adopting new ways, laying the base for a major civilization of their own. In 725 B.C. the kingdom of Kush, centered around a city called Napata, grew in power and wealth to the point that it conquered Egypt itself. The Kushite civilization lived for nearly a thousand years, leaving extensive but still largely unexcavated ruins of its cities and monuments.

About 1500 B.C., Africans to the north, east, and south of the Sahara were agriculturalists, enjoying a reasonably affluent life in villages and small towns. These people were skilled workers in stone, producing refined, polished tools, jewelry, and art objects. In their development they were less sophisticated than the Egyptians and Kushites, but they were probably well ahead of most of the peoples of Europe at that time.

Still farther south, most of Africa was inhabited by

less highly developed people—the aboriginal Khoisan peoples. They knew no agriculture but lived a frugal life hunting, fishing, and gathering roots, berries, and fruits.

Down from the Nile region, in eastern Africa, were other agricultural groups of Africans. Some of these were semi-Negroid peoples more closely related to the modern Ethiopians than to the Bantu people of modern East Africa. These Africans lived in communities around the great mountains and lakes of East Africa, where soils and rainfall are good.

Two thousand years ago, about the time Jesus Christ was born in Palestine, vast changes had been taking place in Africa. Egypt had entered a period of slow decline. Conquered by many successive empires, it was in Roman hands under the rule of the Ptolemies. Rome also had completely destroyed the great North African city of Carthage, and Roman colonies and military bases were established all along the Mediterranean shores of Africa.

By A.D. 200 Kush was just starting on a gradual decline from its period of might. The Kushites were Negroid Africans. They were a successful farming and herding people, but their land did not have quite the same fortunate combination of soil and water factors that produced great wealth so early in Egypt's history. For countless centuries the Kushites were neighbors of the sophisticated Egyptians, trading with them and learning from them—but always at a disadvantage.

For more than a thousand years Egypt had been sorely pressed by wealthy and ambitious neighbors in Asia Minor. Wars weakened Egypt and drained its resources. Kush, buffered by Egypt and separated from the rest of the world by hundreds of miles of harsh terrain, slowly gathered strength. By the eighth century B.C., Kushite forces from Napata had conquered all of Egypt, and for nearly a century the Kushites were the leaders of most of the civilized world. But finally the powerful Assyrians invaded Egypt, and by 600 B.C. the Kushites began to retreat up the Nile to their own homeland.

Meroe, the new capital of Kush, lay at the center of an area rich in iron deposits and fuel for smelting the iron. The Kushites built the city of Meroe into a great mining and ironworking center. From 500 B.C. to A.D. 200 Meroe held sway over a wide empire that drew much of its power from the quantities of tools and weapons that Kushite craftsmen produced. Today the vast ruins of Meroe are surrounded by mountainous slag heaps that attest to its industrial might.

The Kushite state based at Meroe was an African civilization that had borrowed much from Egypt, just as Rome borrowed from Greece and early Europe borrowed from Rome. After its brief imperial venture as the conqueror of Egypt, Kush settled into a long period as a great power in interior Africa. Even though much research must be done before a detailed understanding of Kush's history is possible, it clearly remained wealthy and powerful for many centuries.

Many scholars believe that Kush exercised a great influence on the development of civilization in other parts of Africa. They argue, for example, that such ideas as divine kingship spread from Egypt to Kush, then on to groups all the way across the Sudanic grasslands that rim the southern edge of the Sahara. The legends and traditions of the Ashanti, Hausa, Yoruba, and many other peoples say that their ancestors came originally from the east, some say from Egypt or Arabia. While this is hardly likely, some authorities believe the legends may refer to nobles migrating from Kush to found states in western Africa.

This view is disputed by many other scholars, especially in recent years, who point out that there is very little solid evidence. They note that virtually no coins, pottery, or metal objects of Kushite origin have been found in the western Sudan, and that there is very little real cultural similarity between the two areas.

The case for Kushite influence on the rest of Africa is far from solid. Further, the great cultural achievements of the western Sudan would seem to owe more to local environmental and historical conditions than to borrowing from other peoples.

The earliest Sudanic culture of which much is known is called Nok, because the first evidence of its works was unearthed in the area of Nok in central Nigeria. The peoples of the Nok culture were accomplished workers in stone, terra-cotta, and clay, and left behind them lovely works of art and jewelry from these materials. They learned to mine, smelt, and work iron. Their land was rich in gold, and their descendants built empires on their control of gold production.

The Nok culture may have been widely spread in the Sudanic area, although too little archeological research has been done to be sure. By the time of Christ the whole Sudanic area was flourishing. Its peoples were developing a trade pattern across the Sahara with the Berbers and Romans on the north. Out of this prosper-

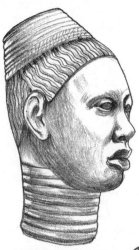

TERRA-COTTA, IFE,
WESTERN NIGERIA

TERRA-COTTA, NOK,
NORTHERN NIGERIA

BRONZE, BENIN,
MID-WESTERN NIGERIA

CALABASH, NIGERIA

GOLD WEIGHT, GHANA

WATER JUG
MANGBETU, ZAIRE

DRINKING CUP
BAKUBA, ZAIRE

ity and trade was to grow, a few centuries later, the first great African empire south of the Sahara: the fabled ancient empire of Ghana.

Although the evidence is not entirely clear, most scholars now agree that it was from the Sudanic area—perhaps from south of Lake Chad—that the Bantu-speaking Africans originated. They spread over most of the central and southern portions of the continent and dramatically changed the history of the land.

In 1500 B.C. the ancestors of the Bantu-speaking peoples were probably a tribe, or a group of tribes, living in the grassland areas somewhere in the general vicinity of the Nigeria-Cameroon border. By the time of Christ they were on the move. They multiplied rapidly into scores of tribes, clans, and nations, conquering all as they spread south and east. These Africans were skilled farmers and herders, good miners and metalworkers, and capable in political and military organization. They moved through the highland and grassland areas into modern Zaire, Zambia, and East Africa, but they were prevented from settling the rain forest and river valley areas because no suitable food crops could be raised there. (The introduction of the banana, yam, and coco yam a few centuries later was to change this.)

On the eastern side of Africa at the time of Christ, a small, strong state had developed in what is now northern Ethiopia, around the city of Axum. Located hundreds of miles up the Blue Nile from Meroe, in fertile lands on the high plateau, the state of Axum was expanding and was already engaged in trade—and probably occasional hostilities—with Kush.

Not many years later, Meroe became a haven and a center of missionary work for early Christian believers. Christianity spread from Meroe into Nubia, Darfur, and Axum. In the fourth century the rulers of Axum adopted Christianity, establishing the Coptic Christian Church, which has continued into modern times.

Even before Axum became Christian, it was powerful and wealthy. Gradually it overshadowed Meroe as the great center of Africa's trade with Egypt, Greece, and Asia. Finally it sent its armies down the Nile and destroyed Meroe and other Kushite towns.

For several centuries afterward, Axum enjoyed a position of unrivaled power and influence. Its craftsmen built great stone obelisks and monuments, and later huge churches were carved out of the stone mountains. The people terraced their hillsides and used irrigation to sustain large crops. Axum traded African ivory, gold, feathers, hides, spices, and iron in return for cloth, jewelry, and other foreign goods.

In the process of trading goods with the rest of the world, Axum also exchanged diplomats and scholars— but for all too brief a period. Axum's priests and pilgrims traveled regularly in Christian areas of Egypt and Palestine. Axumite ambassadors maintained liaison with Rome, Constantinople, Alexandria, Athens, and Damascus. But the lofty highlands of Axum eventually became isolated from the mainstream of world civilization. Axum sank into a medieval era from which it has begun to emerge only in the past century.

Along the coast of eastern Africa at the time of Christ, an important alien influence was beginning to be felt. Arab seafarers were venturing farther south, past the Horn of Africa, and establishing small trading colonies and ports—often on the islands just off the coast. There they made contact and traded with the newly arrived Bantu-speaking peoples. Within a few centuries, the Arab settlements would blend into the native African scene, contributing to the development of such power-

OBELISK, AXUM

ful trading cities as Sofala, Mozambique; Kilwa, Tanzania; and Malindi, Kenya.

Thus, in the Africa of the early Christian era, Egypt was in decline and under Roman sway. Meroe, though still the center of a far-flung Kushite power, was beginning to lose its wealth and influence to the rapidly growing power of Axum. Both Axum and Meroe were trading with, and influencing, the peoples of the highlands of eastern and east-central Africa. These peoples in turn were in contact with Arab seafarers at several points along the Indian Ocean coast.

In western Africa, all along the southern edge of the Sahara, and in the great central grasslands between the Niger and Nile rivers, a great Sudanic civilization was developing and spreading. Its peoples were beginning to trade with the peoples living on the fringes of the rain forests, and with northern Africa through several Saharan caravan routes. One branch of the Sudanic peoples, the Bantu, had moved southward to the east and south of the great rain forest of the Congo basin; and from that area they were settling the lake and mountain regions of eastern Africa and the highlands of southern Africa.

In the next thousand years Africa changed much. Egypt and Kush declined into relative obscurity; Axum still held sway in the Ethiopian highlands but was now surrounded by Islamic states which, though not unfriendly, isolated it from its former relationship with the outside world; northern Africa was rapidly coming

under the control of Islam; and the great Sudanic civilization had established itself as the moving force in almost all of Africa south of the Sahara.

The Sudanic civilization in A.D. 1000 was at its apex,
in the empire of Ghana. But Sudanic peoples eventually
established city-states in many other areas: along the
Niger and Senegal rivers, around Lake Chad, on the
south side of the Congo River, in the Angola and Shaba
(Katanga) regions, in the Rhodesian highlands, and
around the great lakes of eastern Africa. Mingling with
the Arab settlers along the Indian Ocean coast, peoples
originating from the Sudanic area helped to build a
string of powerful seaports at Sofala, Mtwara, Kilwa,
Zanzibar, Mombasa, and Malindi.

Africa was largely cut off from Europe during the
European medieval period. But it maintained a continuous relationship with the Islamic civilization as well as
an uninterrupted trade with India and China. The best
source of information about Africa in those days is the
accounts left by Arab travelers who visited African cities
and empires and who wrote glowingly of their wealth
and enlightenment.

Ghana was founded, probably between A.D. 200 and
400, in the western Sudan area between the Senegal
and Niger rivers. It began as the empire of Aoukar; but
gradually it became known as Ghana, from the indigenous word for "king," by which its rulers were widely
known. As an empire, Ghana existed for nearly ten
centuries.

The kings who originally conquered surrounding
peoples to create the empire of Ghana had two important aids: their knowledge of ironworking and the strategic location of their territory.

The empire of Ghana was built by Soninke peoples.
Their lands lay at the southern ends of the caravan

routes of the western Sahara. The Soninke maintained peaceful relations with the desert Berbers, who supplied salt and various northern African goods, and with other Sudanic peoples who produced gold, copper, and trade goods for northern Africa. Strong in themselves because of their ironworking techniques and the weapons they could thus produce, the Soninke kings also took advantage of the trade routes across their territory. In return for a guarantee of safe conduct, they collected duties on all goods entering and leaving the kingdom.

The kings of Ghana gained control of a vast area, stretching from the Senegal River east to the Niger River, and north well into the Sahara. Al-Bakri, an eleventh-century Arab scholar, wrote that the Ghanaian king, Tenkaminin, could field an army of 200,000 troops. This, obviously, is how Ghana was able to guarantee peace and security to the traders who traveled great distances with their valuable goods, so long as they obeyed Ghana's laws and paid their taxes. Various accounts of ancient Ghana, especially those of the eleventh and twelfth centuries, stress its good government, its power—but especially its wealth.

The empire of Ghana continued in power well into the eleventh century. But about 1054 Ghana's northernmost city, Audoghost, fell to an army of Berbers from what is now Mauritania, who were zealous Moslems engaged in a "jihad," or holy war, against all non-Moslems. Although Moslem traders and scholars were welcome in Ghana's cities and built settlements there, the empire was always ruled by kings who practiced their own traditional religion. In 1076 the Berber invaders—called the Almoravids—captured the capital, and the Ghanaian empire began to break apart. The Almoravids were never able to reunite the empire, and

Ghana gradually faded into obscurity as a force in western Africa.

The Almoravids, an impoverished but fierce group of Berbers, also swept north and conquered Morocco at about the same time they marched against Ghana. From Morocco they launched a successful invasion of Portugal and Spain. They seem to have been considerably more successful in northern Africa and southern Europe than in western Africa.

Ghana was not the only case of Sudanic growth in Africa of the year 1000. The state of Kanem, to the east of Lake Chad, was coming into existence at the same time. In league with the state of Bornu, it developed into a powerful empire that lasted nearly seven hundred years. The cities that later produced the Mali and Songhay empires were active in 1000. A powerful state was being established by the Bakongo people in the region of modern Zaire and Angola. The Shaba (Katanga) area of modern Zaire and Zambia was settled by mining peoples, the Baluba and Balunda, who a few centuries later developed another strong state.

The Shaba (Katanga) area, a major copper producer

ZIMBABWE RUINS

then as now, was involved in trade with the outside world through the eastern African ports that the Arabs had established. Sofala was the most active of these port cities, and it conducted a thriving commerce in gold and ivory as well as copper. Gold and ivory came to Sofala from a great state, known by reputation to the Arab scholars of the day, in the African interior. Almost certainly it was this state that left the great stone ruins of Zimbabwe.

The Africa of A.D. 1000 was a land of great vitality. In the interior areas, where few non-Africans ever ventured, there were large towns, budding empires, well-developed trade patterns, widespread mining and metalworking, and ambitious military movements. The empire of Ghana is at least partially described in Arabic literature, as are Sofala and other eastern African port cities. The empire of Axum left records written by its own scholars. But of the great ferment and growth taking place from Lake Chad down to Angola, and from the Congo forests across to eastern Africa, there are today only a few tantalizing hints gleaned from archeological studies, tales passed from generation to generation, and chance references in Arabic, Indian, and Chinese works of the period.

Between 1000 and 1850 there was continuous growth in the power of the Sudanic states and empires, in the Arab Moslem influence, and eventually in communication and trade with Europe. This period was the golden age of most of Africa. Important centers of trade, industry, and scholarship flourished over the entire Sudanic world, as far south as the modern Republic of South Africa.

After Ghana split apart in the twelfth century, various states that had been provinces of Ghana tried to exert their might over neighboring states, in an attempt to build new empires and to monopolize the still-rich trans-Saharan trade. By 1203 a king of the Fulani peoples, Sumanguru, had taken Ghana's last capital, Kumbi. At some time between 1230 and 1240 he sent his troops against the small state of Kangaba, home of the Mandinka people. Led by Sundiata Keita, a chief whose name is still revered in the legends of western Africa, the Kangaba army defeated the Fulanis, killed Sumanguru, and seized enough power to start the new empire of Mali.

Over a period of about twenty years, Sundiata Keita conquered a number of neighboring states. His successors continued to make small conquests from 1255 until 1312, when Mansa Musa came to power. Mansa Musa was the greatest of Mali's emperors. During the twenty years of his reign he expanded the empire's territory more than fivefold, making it nearly twice as large as the empire of Ghana had been.

There are few written records that tell in detail of life in ancient Mali. One North African scholar, Ibn Khaldun, visited Mali and was welcomed by Mansa Musa. Ibn Khaldun and other writers were impressed by Mali's great wealth in gold and by the peace and order that prevailed over a territory so large that it took weeks to traverse it.

Certain Mali cities, notably Timbuktu and Gao, that were rich and powerful are still in existence. Mansa Musa attracted to Mali a number of scholars from northern Africa. Centers of learning developed, and in a few cases these led to the establishment of universities. Mansa Musa sent ambassadors to Morocco and Egypt and received ambassadors from both countries.

In 1324 Mansa Musa, a devout Moslem, made a pilgrimage to the city of Mecca in Arabia. In his caravan were thousands of people, many of them slaves bearing food and gold. It is said that Mansa Musa spent so much gold in Cairo, when he stopped there, that the city suffered a period of serious inflation.

But Mansa Musa's successors were not strong enough to keep the empire of Mali intact. One after another of its subject states revolted; and although some of the revolts were put down, the empire began to crumble about 1400. Fierce bands of Tuareg warriors, for many years kept at bay by the fear of Mali's well-armed and disciplined troops, began to sweep out of the desert to attack Mali trade caravans and cities. About 1550 Mali had declined to a small state of little influence.

As Mali declined, it was superseded by the empire of Songhay. The capital and heart of Songhay was the city of Gao, which was an important trade center as early as 1000. Gao and the surrounding area grew gradually into a major metropolis of commerce and learning. Conquered by Mali about 1325, it was not content to be a subject state in the Mali empire and broke free in 1375. For nearly a century the Songhay peoples of Gao maintained their independence as a small city-state. In 1464, however, an ambitious ruler named Sunni Ali came to power. When he died in 1492, Songhay was an empire that rivaled Mali.

Songhay's most extensive expansion began in 1493, when Askia Muhammad assumed the throne. During his reign the empire tripled in size, eventually covering an area as large as ancient Ghana and Mali combined. At its peak the empire of Songhay stretched from the Atlantic Ocean coast of what is now Guinea eastward into parts of modern Niger and Nigeria.

The golden age of Songhay lasted only a little over a century. In 1591 Moroccan troops, well organized and armed with guns, marched across the Sahara and invaded Songhay. Swiftly their superior weapons enabled them to capture Timbuktu and Gao, Songhay's two chief cities, and the empire collapsed.

Other states, not so large or wealthy as Mali and Songhay, grew up over much of Africa south of the Sahara. Most of these states were built in grassland and highland areas, where the grains that the Sudanic peoples grew could flourish.

Between 1000 and 1850, western Africa saw the rise to power of the Hausa states, notably Kano, Gobir, Katsina, Kebbi, and Zaria. These states were wealthy and civilized, but they were never able to unite into an empire. (The city-states of Bornu and Kanem did unite into an empire, of long life and vast area.) There were other states in the interior part of western Africa that were strong enough to keep out of the hands of the kings of Mali, Songhay, and Kanem-Bornu. These included the several Mossi states of what is now northern Ghana and Upper Volta, and the states of Nupe, Jukun, and Oyo, in Nigeria.

About 1400, other important states appeared deep in the rain-forest area included by the modern nations of Ivory Coast, Ghana, and Nigeria. Here the Akan-speaking peoples had spread across a wide area. One of these peoples, the Ashanti, built a small state on the edge of the forests in what is modern Ghana, where it was safe from the powerful cavalry of the states of the grasslands. Later it was to grow into a powerful empire.

During this period the Yoruba people, at one time centered in the state of Oyo, penetrated the great forests of southern Nigeria and built populous cities there. Ibadan, the greatest Yoruba city, exists today; it is the largest totally African city south of the Sahara. A variety of smaller states grew up in the Niger River delta and along the coast of Guinea.

Less is known about the Sudanic states that developed in central, southern, and eastern Africa. When the Portuguese first established themselves on the Mozambique coast, they soon found evidence of the kingdom of Monomotapa along the Zambezi River, and they heard of powerful kings farther into the interior. At Zimbabwe an early people left magnificent stone structures. The Baluba people of Shaba (Katanga) controlled a large inland mining area. Sudanic-type states existed from the vicinity of what is now the Republic of South Africa north to the lands of modern Uganda.

Century by century the history of Europe has gone on, from achievement to greater achievement. The history of Africa, on the other hand, seems to indicate a much slower climb—indeed, a leveling off that has lasted for centuries. Why?

The African land—the physical environment—has had a powerful influence on the kinds of civilizations that Africans have produced. Certain portions of the land were favorable to man's progress, indeed more favorable than the land of Europe. In the fertile delta of the Nile and along the well-watered banks of that great river, Africans were able to achieve a prosperous life for themselves while the peoples of Europe were battling a frugal environment. Great civilizations were born and flourished along the Nile.

But in most of Africa, the land yielded only enough food and resources to support a gradually increasing, moderately prosperous population. It could not support and sustain a rise in wealth and power for the many.

The civilizations of Ghana, Mali, and Songhay are excellent cases in point. By the time of Christ, and for a few centuries afterward, inland western Africa had enough food, gold, and iron to support a population at a level that compared favorably with the level in Europe at the same time. There was enough wealth from the land to permit some men to rise to prominence, supported by the wealth of their fellows. In turn, the wealth of these men was sufficient to raise and maintain armies to conquer and control all the grassland areas of the western Sudan region.

The power of Ghana was great, and it lasted for many centuries. But it was not great enough to accomplish the two things that make for an expanding civilization: the conquest of surrounding territories that add new sources of wealth for the original empire; and the development of better ways to produce wealth within the central area.

Ghana was bordered on the north by the inhospitable Sahara Desert, and on the south by the great rain forests. For all its power and wealth, Ghana was not strong enough to cross the Sahara to tap the resources of northern Africa and southern Europe, or to conquer the peoples of the forests for their gold, timber, and food.

The land of ancient Ghana was of limited fertility and

water resources. The people of Ghana developed ways of coaxing from the land as much as it could produce, but they were able to do no more. Thus they prospered enough to build a powerful empire—but not enough to increase its power continuously from within.

Ghana became, as did Mali and Songhay after it, a captive of the physical environment where it developed. It could not produce more people and more wealth than the land would afford.

Egypt and Kush thrived in environments that could support dense populations and great wealth. Rome and Greece were able to push beyond their own limited environment, across the surrounding country and the Mediterranean Sea, to conquer other peoples and acquire wealth that their own lands would not produce. But western Africa had neither the enormous internal resources of Egypt nor the access to surrounding wealth of Rome and Greece.

The evidence is that the civilization of western Africa reached the height of possible development with the empire of Ghana. There was little further advancement during the following centuries of the Mali and Songhay empires. Moslem scholars brought writing; but the lives of the people changed little. Apart from the intellectual contribution of the Moslems, western Africa was largely isolated from the discoveries in science and technology that were taking place in Europe from the Renaissance onward.

The skills and wisdom of the men who built and maintained Ghana, Mali, Songhay, and other African states and civilizations were as great as the skills of any leaders of Europe and Asia. Vast armies were assembled, trained, and led to victory. Effective systems of government, law, and communication were developed to unite, in peace and tranquility, great empires. Works of art were produced. But these achievements, great though they were, could not totally transform an environment nor remove limitations such as the Sahara Desert.

All of Africa south of the Sahara, like western Africa, was imprisoned by its environment. A much higher level of civilization existed there than the Western world has been aware of. Africa has a history—a history containing proud moments and illustrious chapters. But the people could not break through the limitations of their environment to participate fully in the progress of science and technology that has changed the faces of Europe and America.

The shackles that Africa's environment imposed on its history have been broken now by the coming of European science and technology. Europe has grievously exploited Africa, so that its contribution to African development has been detrimental as well as helpful. But now that Africa is free of colonial rule, it has the chance to use the best of the European legacy to create another, and greater, golden age of the future.

◀ 5 ▶

Europe Discovers Africa: The Colonial Conquest

The huge Sahara Desert and the great oceans sealed off most of Africa from direct contact with Europe until venturesome Portuguese mariners visited western Africa in the fifteenth century. To the Europe of that day Africa, beyond the Mediterranean shores and the lower Nile of Egypt, was the great unknown. Europe knew even less of events in Africa than Africa knew of events in Europe.

Africa had influenced the outside world. Egyptian ideas of the nature of the universe, and in science and technology, had had great effect on Greece, Rome, Minos, and early European civilization. African gold, ivory, hides, and spices were important in the world economy. The Moors of northern Africa, through their conquest of Spain and Portugal, had great cultural impact. The Arabs, Indians, and (for a time) the Chinese had continuous trade with eastern Africa after the time of Christ.

But it was the hardy mariners of fifteenth-century Portugal who "discovered" Africa for Europe. European seamen before this time had heard tales of the mysterious land of the black men and its gold and ivory; but they had no charts, compasses, or sails to run into the wind. The few who set out into the Atlantic before the prevailing winds never returned. But in the early fifteenth century Portugal learned the use of Indian lateen sails from the Arabs, acquired Chinese navigation devices, and began to chart the unknown. Before the end of the century, the coasts of Africa were known; trade had started; and a new era had begun for both Europe and Africa.

Through most of the fifteenth century, the Portuguese jealously guarded their knowledge of Africa and of their routes to India and China. But it was not long before the Dutch, British, Danes, and French were exploring too. The Spanish, great adventurers of the same period, devoted such attention to their conquest of the Americas that they had scant time for Africa. By the middle of the sixteenth century there was a lively trade between various European nations and western Africa, and European trading posts and forts had been established at strategic points all around the continent.

Just as the Portuguese pioneered in opening the routes to western Africa, so they were the first to lay claim to eastern Africa. But on the eastern side of the continent they met resistance from the Arabs, who had dominated the area for centuries, and also from the Turks. The Portuguese built forts and persevered; but they were gradually pushed southward by both Arabs and Ottoman Turks to the coast of Mozambique, which they held until 1974.

On the western side of Africa, the heavily populated coast between the mouth of the Senegal River and the area of Angola attracted increasing numbers of European ships, eager to trade European cloth, guns, and utensils for the pepper, ivory, gold, and vegetable oils of the area. Treaties were negotiated with the coastal African kings, and trading bases were established. Then, in the sixteenth century, the traders of Europe began to exploit an even richer commodity: slaves for the sugar plantations of the New World. For nearly four centuries a vast flow of human cargo passed from the coasts of Africa to the Americas. Both the trade in goods and the trade in slaves had far-reaching effects on the balance of power in Africa and on its course of development.

The early Portuguese mariners, and the other Europeans who followed them, were not in the main scholarly adventurers or disinterested explorers. Europe was just emerging from a long sleep—the Middle Ages. The wealthier and better-educated people and the nobility were avid for luxuries—for spices, for gold, and for exotic objects. For centuries there had been only a trickle of these goods from the caravans of Asia and Africa.

Europe eagerly seized its new skill at navigation to answer the demand for a greater supply of goods. New sea routes were also desired because Arab Moslems controlled the access to the prized African and Asian goods, and they were not friendly suppliers to the hated Christian Europeans. Africa was equally cut off from the European goods it sought, by the Sahara and by the Arabs who controlled northern Africa.

The powerful Sudanic states of the sub-Saharan grasslands had long enriched themselves from their monopoly of trade across the Sahara. Gold flowed from western Africa to Mali, Songhay, and Kanem-Bornu, and in return there was salt from the Sahara, cloth, beads, and occasional specialty goods—guns, clocks, books—from northern Africa and Europe.

When European and African trade interests came into direct contact, the Sudanic states began to lose their monopoly—the root of their wealth and power. The formerly weak coastal states and their neighbors farther inland became the new masters of trade. Until the sixteenth and seventeenth centuries it was the far interior of western Africa that had flourished. From those times to the present, the coastal and forest states have grown and prospered while the interior has declined.

The new trade slowly changed Africa's balance of power. In western Africa, where the change was most pronounced, formerly small states armed themselves with guns and began to expand—and new empires appeared. The Ashanti, for example, gradually expanded their territory from the center of what is modern Ghana, bringing under their control northern Ghana and large chunks of what are now Togo and the Ivory Coast. In eastern and Central Africa the early trade in goods had less effect; but the later trade in slaves had severe impact.

One neglected feature of the trade in goods is that it first brought distilled alcoholic beverages to Africa. Many an African king, once he and his court learned the "delights" of Europe's distilled spirits, traded large measures of gold, ivory, and slaves for a few small casks of brandy and rum.

Africans were no more nor less gullible than anyone

else, but they had no standards by which to measure the true worth of the European goods they bought. Cloth, produced cheaply in Europe, brought high prices in Africa—as did alcoholic spirits, inferior clocks and instruments, and antiquated secondhand guns. On the other hand, many African kings set laws that strictly regulated the activities of the European traders, and the values of goods were stipulated after careful study and thought. In some areas Europeans who brought inferior goods or charged exorbitant prices were punished or banned from doing further trade. Despite the fact that Europe got the better of the bargain, some African states prospered on the trade, and the balance of African power shifted.

The Europe of the sixteenth and seventeenth centuries was curious and greedy for the wonders and riches across the seas. Although Europe was interested in Africa, it was even more interested in the New World and "the Indies" of the East. Early Spanish and Portuguese voyages to the Americas brought back ships laden with gold and jewels, and rumors of much greater riches still undiscovered. From the East they brought a variety of spices, jewels, delicate art works, and silks. Within a few decades the British, Danes, Dutch, French, and other Europeans were sallying forth in great numbers to share in the spoils.

Africa proved less rewarding than the East and the Americas. Gold, ivory, and spices could be obtained, but not always in lavish abundance. Some African kings were hostile, and strong enough to make most European ships give their coasts a wide berth. And Africa's climate and diseases took a heavy toll of Europeans who lingered long onshore.

Then the traffic in slaves began, and the pattern of trade was revolutionized. Slavery had existed in western Africa before the first Europeans arrived. The Moslems of northern Africa had long looked southward, as well as to Europe, for the slaves they so highly prized. Africans themselves used slaves. For many centuries the kings and the wealthy classes of western African states had owned slaves, acquired when they conquered other peoples. They felt that it was only natural when Europe showed interest in acquiring slaves.

But slavery in Africa had meant something quite different from the new slavery of the European. Slaves in Africa may have been captives, or criminals, or people exiled from their own country because of bad behavior —but they were still human beings, with a certain security and status. African slaves could marry and keep their spouses and children with them. They could, and sometimes did, rise to high positions if their talents warranted. Slavery in Africa was evil; but as an institution it never reached the depths of inhumanity that characterized European slavery in the New World.

During the sixteenth century the slave trade was relatively small. It was carried on almost entirely by the Portuguese. The Portuguese and the Spanish used slaves in limited numbers in Portugal and Spain. Then they began to use increasing numbers in Central and South America. It is estimated that roughly 900,000 slaves were taken from Africa by the Portuguese during the sixteenth century—an average of 9,000 each year.

The colonization of the West Indies by the British, Dutch, and French in the seventeenth century created a new need for labor in the sugar plantations there. The native Indians made poor laborers for the plantations. They were unused to the sustained daily labor required to make sugar profitable; their attitudes toward forced labor, or slavery, were negative; and they died in droves when first exposed to European diseases. When pressed into service, they often rebelled. Yet sugar was in great demand in Europe, and European labor was expensive and in short supply. Africa's millions provided the unwholesome answer.

The Africans who lived along the Atlantic Ocean coast were hardy people who were used to heavy work in hot climates. They had resistance to many of the European diseases. Because slavery and hard work were well known to them, they were able, when taken as slaves to the West Indies, to adapt to the harsh conditions and still produce. They relished becoming slaves no more than other human beings; but when they had no alternative, they could survive and even maintain their sense of humanity.

During the sixteenth century, the Portuguese were masters of much of Africa's coastal trade. But as the slave trade grew, the British, Dutch, and French began to shoulder the Portuguese aside. By the early seventeenth century, the French had monopolized the area around the mouth of the Senegal River; the Dutch and the British had taken over the Gold Coast and the Slave Coast (as the shore from the Gold Coast to the Niger delta soon came to be called); and the Portuguese held on to a few small posts, largely confined to the Congo area and eastern African coast. In the seventeenth century the traffic in slaves trebled at least. Roughly three million people arrived to be sold in the slave markets of the Americas.

As active as the slave trade was, it accelerated in the eighteenth century, when the cotton plantations of the North American colonies added their labor demands to those of the sugar plantations. Decade after decade, America's South was opened and settled—and cotton was to become king there. To produce cotton the settlers needed cheap labor—and labor that could survive constant exertion in a warm climate. The African slaves, already used to advantage in the West Indies, provided the solution.

In the eighteenth century more than five million slaves were landed alive in the Americas. The records of the slavers tell us that great numbers of captives died on their way from the interior to the coastal slave markets in Africa; many others were killed or left to starve in slave raids and wars waged to capture slaves; and still countless others perished in the tightly packed slave ships as they were transported across the Atlantic.

For nearly four centuries the loathsome traffic in African slaves flourished. Well over 10 million slaves were landed and sold in the New World—uprooted from their own land and their families, shackled and

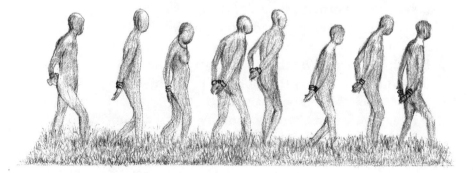

branded like cattle, and condemned to a life of incessant labor and hardship. Some authorities have estimated that the slave trade removed from Africa, by capture, death, or starvation, more than 70 million human beings. The population of Africa was prevented from increasing at least partly as a result of what has been called "this human hemorrhage"—while that of the rest of the world increased. In the eighteenth century Africans constituted about one fifth of the world's population. Today they are about one twelfth.

Paradoxically, the slave trade produced the least permanent population disturbance where it was heaviest: along the Guinea Gulf in the area that is now Benin and Nigeria. This area is today among the most densely populated in Africa. The worst effects of slavery on population were experienced in what are now Gabon, Congo, Angola, and Tanzania. (The last suffered from a different slave trade—that operated by the Arabs of Arabia and the Middle East.)

The Africans did not accept slavery complacently. The worst toll of the slave trade was the millions killed in the wars fought to resist being taken as slaves. The slave-trading kingdoms along the coast and in the interior, especially those with guns, had the power to conquer inland peoples and take slaves. But these peoples

resisted valiantly, some even suffering total destruction in the process.

Many of the kings who captured and sold slaves eventually sickened of slavery's foul consequences. In the early sixteenth century King Affonso of the Bakongo state, in alliance with King John of Portugal, wrote a poignant series of letters to King John protesting the growing slave trade in his kingdom. But the Portuguese persisted, and the trade grew. The Bakongo state, powerful enough by African standards, did not have the power to stop the detested trade.

In those days as later, Africa was a series of independent states and kingdoms. Up and down the African coast some of the wiser and more humane kings spurned the slave trade. However, slavers managed to find alternative sources from less scrupulous kings.

The Africans sold into slavery often revolted either on the ships, when they could, or in America after they arrived. Early American history records a never-ending series of minor revolts, of escapes into the forests, and even of suicides by proud men who preferred death to a life of slavery. But the trade grew. Today more than 25 million black Americans, plus millions of other people in the West Indies and South America, bear living witness to the trade's size and tenure, and to the African's ability to survive against enormous odds under cruel circumstances.

Another slave trade flourished in eastern Africa, lasting into the twentieth century. For centuries the Arabs of the coastal towns of eastern Africa, and their African allies, forayed inland to capture slaves for the markets of the East. When the Portuguese established themselves in Mozambique, they too engaged in this trade. Except for a flow of Mozambican slaves to Brazil, the eastern African trade was largely to the markets of

Arabia, Turkey, India, Madagascar, and Indian Ocean islands.

The eastern African slave trade never reached the size of that in western Africa; but it was, if anything, even more brutal and inhuman. In the nineteenth century Dr. David Livingstone, the celebrated explorer and missionary, traveled extensively through the area of slaving operations in Tanganyika and described them fully. The Arab and Swahili slavers, operating from base camps in the interior, devastated town after town in their search for captives. Once captured, the slaves were tied together and forced to carry ivory and other goods on the long, dangerous journey to the coast. Often more died on this cruel journey than reached the sea—but human lives were cheap to the slavers. In Tanganyika, as in other parts of eastern and central Africa, enormous areas were depopulated. Only in the past fifty years have people begun to live in these areas again.

For most of Africa the horrors of the slave trade ended in the middle of the nineteenth century, when England and the United States outlawed slavery and belatedly used their power to stop the trade. But it continued in eastern Africa into the early twentieth century, after the colonial era had begun. In other parts of Africa—notably the Belgian Congo and Portuguese Africa—the trade in slaves was eradicated, but various other forms of forced labor and human exploitation took its place.

Europe's discovery of Africa led to five hundred years of interaction that had mixed consequences for Africa. The ideas and tools that Africa needed to participate in the scientific and technological revolution that was sweeping the rest of the world were slowly acquired from Europe. But in return Europe exacted a heavy toll —in slaves, in minerals, and in the products of the African land. The slave trade and the long pattern of economic exploitation have left a bitter legacy in Africa.

Until the last decade of the eighteenth century, the European adventure in Africa was confined almost exclusively to the coasts. For roughly three hundred and fifty years Europe sent its ships to Africa, developed patterns of trade, caused misery and fundamental shifts in power through the slave traffic—but had virtually no inkling of the vast interior of the continent. No European had seen the Niger River except at the delta, which was not recognized as the river's mouth. Yet along the Niger great cities, states, and empires had come and gone for more than fifteen centuries. No European knew of the immense highland areas that run from Ethiopia to the southern tip of Africa. The source of the Nile River was a dark mystery.

There were three reasons for Europe's confinement to the coasts. First, European interest in Africa was more commercial than intellectual. There was little motivation to explore beyond the coastal markets. Second, the heat and diseases found on Africa's coasts were effective deterrents. Europeans did not always survive ventures into the threatening interior, and most visitors did not want to take the risk. Third, and perhaps most important, the coastal Africans discouraged European travel into the interior, because they were anxious to maintain their monopoly over the supply of goods and slaves that the Europeans wanted. The coastal kings and their neighbors immediately behind them, thriving on the profits from the trade, were aware that the well-armed, skillful Europeans could strike bargains directly with the interior kings if they had access.

Much was happening in the African interior that was unknown to Europe. Mali was in a period of decline, and Songhay was shattered after having been invaded by Morocco. But the most dramatic events in the interior during the seventeenth and eighteenth centuries took place in the great rain forests and in the drier areas just to their north. Here several states that had been relatively weak in the past grew strong and extended their power in all directions. One of the most notable of these new powers was that of the Ashanti, a group speaking the Twi language of the large Akan linguistic subfamily.

The Ashanti began to develop as a nation toward the middle of the seventeenth century, when a group of Twi-speaking peoples who lived near the site of modern Kumasi, Ghana, formed a loose union and named themselves Ashanti. About the end of the seventeenth century, all the Ashanti and other Twi-speaking relatives were united into a closely knit nation. Though united, the Ashanti were nonetheless under the overlordship of the king of the Denkyira state.

Securing a good supply of guns and ammunition from the great Dutch trading post at Elmina on the coast, Osei Tutu, the "asantahene" (king) of the Ashanti peoples, overthrew the Denkyira king and proclaimed Ashanti independence. He and other asantahene after him expanded Ashanti into a sizable empire that covered most of modern Ghana and extended into parts of what are now Ivory Coast and Togo.

The Ashanti empire reigned supreme for nearly two hundred years until 1900, when it was subjugated by

British forces. It had continual contact with the Dutch at Elmina, the British (who ousted the Dutch from Elmina), and the Danes; but these Europeans knew little of Ashanti until the nineteenth century.

When the American colonies seized their independence in 1776 and emerged as a free nation, British interest in preserving the flow of slaves to America declined. England no longer had responsibility for America nor shared its profits. Liberal voices had long been raised in England against slavery, but they met stiff opposition until the United States broke free. Then the antislavery forces became stronger, and the British slave trade was finally abolished in 1807. There appeared in the period between about 1780 and 1820 a significant nucleus of Christian liberals, scientists, and geographers who wanted to learn about Africa and to help its peoples.

In the early years of the nineteenth century a similar process was going on in France, Germany, Holland, the United States, and other countries. One after another joined Britain in outlawing the slave trade—and in looking at Africa with new eyes.

In England and other European countries the iniquitous slave trade was the object of Christian protest that led gradually to a broader concern for the welfare of Africa. Protestants at first, then Catholics began to work toward the abolition of slavery and the trade in slaves, then for the Christianization and education of the Africans who had for so long suffered from the slave traffic.

Even before liberal movements could halt the slave trade, they became more aware of the Africans in England, the United States, and (to a lesser extent) France who had gained their freedom from slavery. By the end of the eighteenth century tens of thousands of former slaves in these countries were working in generally menial positions as servants, laborers, and artisans. To assist these freedmen to find a new life for themselves, philanthropic groups in England, and later in the United States, were formed to establish colonies of freedmen back in Africa.

Thus, in 1787, 411 former slaves landed, in company with their English benefactors, on the western African coast to found the colony of Sierra Leone. They purchased land from the Temne king of the area, cut down the bush, and planted crops. The nation of Liberia was founded in 1821, by freed American slaves, a few hundred miles east of Sierra Leone.

Both Sierra Leone and Liberia were started under adverse conditions and were chronically short of funds and skills. In 1808 the British government took over Sierra Leone as a crown colony and ruled the coastal strip inhabited by the freedmen. Later, when Britain established a protectorate over the tribal lands of the interior, the modern country of Sierra Leone took shape.

The American government never took official responsibility for Liberia. The colonists, who became known as Americo-Liberians, were often left to fend for themselves. On a few occasions when Liberia was threatened by European colonial powers (France actually seized—and kept—a portion of Liberia's original territory), the United States came to its aid. But despite adversity, Liberia has maintained its independence since its original founding.

Perhaps even more important than the founding of Sierra Leone and Liberia was the growth of Christian missions in Africa. Missionaries were sent to educate and "civilize" Africans so that they could one day deal with Europeans on a more nearly equal footing. The missions not only brought Western education to Africa for the first time but helped to stimulate European interest in penetrating the interior and opening up the whole continent.

At the beginning of the nineteenth century, most of the Portuguese institutions in Africa, such as the missions, embassies, and trade systems in Bakongo, the Gold Coast, and Gabon, had faded with little trace, although Portugal was established in several parts of Angola and Mozambique. The French were in control around the mouth of the Senegal River. They explored several hundred miles up the river and began to westernize the people of the area. Sierra Leone had been founded, but it was still a tiny outpost with little effect on the rest of Africa. Britain had a lasting foothold along the Gold Coast and in parts of Nigeria and had also spread some Western influence among the coastal Africans of the area. The Dutch farmers on the Cape of Good Hope, who called themselves Boers (from their word for "farmers"), were pressing inland in southern Africa, as were a group of English settlers.

Mungo Park, the intrepid British explorer, had reached the Niger River and visited some of the inland states of western Africa. James Bruce, a Scot, explored the highlands of Ethiopia and reported extensively on Gondar and other states.

Before the nineteenth century ended, all of Africa except for a few remote areas had been mapped, reported on, and opened to Europe. After Mungo Park's expedition, European exploration of Sudanic Africa increased. England's Major Dixon Denham and Captain Hugh Clapperton crossed the Sahara between 1823 and 1825 and visited the countries of Bornu and Hausaland. John and Richard Landers, also British, followed the Niger River to the sea in 1830.

German explorers also were active during the same

period. Heinrich Barth systematically explored most of the central and western Sudan region between 1850 and 1855. Ludwig Krapfs and Johann Rebmann explored the countryside of Kenya between 1847 and 1849. They were the first Europeans to see Africa's highest mountain, Kilimanjaro. Gerhard Rohlfs and Gustav Nachtigal explored much of the Sahara and the area occupied today by Sudan.

One of the most effective and famous African explorers was David Livingstone, a doctor and missionary. He spent over twenty years exploring, establishing missions, and opening travel routes, from South Africa and Bechuanaland up to Tanganyika, the Congo, and Ruanda-Urundi. His travels to the Lake Tanganyika region and the upper Congo River basin, between 1867 and 1873, isolated him from the rest of the world for such a long period that a correspondent for the *New York Herald,* H. M. Stanley, was sent by his newspaper on a now famous trip to find Livingstone.

Stanley himself, after finding Livingstone at Ujiji on Lake Tanganyika, became addicted to African ventures. More than any other man, he opened up the vast Congo area to the West. Eventually he was engaged by King Leopold of Belgium to help establish the Belgian Congo.

The fact that the Nile originates in Lake Victoria was proved by Britain's John Speke in 1862. Other British explorers, notably Captain Richard Burton and Sir Samuel Baker, roamed over eastern Africa and the Sudan in the 1860's and 1870's. This area had long excited Europe's curiosity because of its ivory and the mystery surrounding the source of the Nile.

The European exploration of interior Africa in the nineteenth century was motivated, at least in part, by the humanitarian concern of Europe's Christians and

liberals. Many of the explorers were missionaries or were financed by mission societies. Mission stations, schools, and medical clinics followed soon after the first trails were blazed.

But there was also an economic side to Europe's new interest in Africa. Even though the explorers did not uncover any fabulous new sources of wealth in Africa, they were supported by industrialists and trading concerns that realized that Africa could produce raw materials and could buy more manufactured goods. The Industrial Revolution that was sweeping Europe needed raw materials, and it needed growing markets.

The new economic interest in Africa was only a part of Europe's worldwide search for markets, territories, and spheres of influence. In the latter part of the nineteenth century various European countries were competing with each other on many counts. The seeds of World War I were beginning to grow.

It was this increasing competition among the European powers that changed their trading relationship with Africa, of more than four centuries, into a frantic scramble for pieces of the continent. King Leopold's employment of Stanley to explore the Congo, sign treaties, and establish trading stations was the first dramatic move. Five years of furious activity followed, with money and men pouring into the Congo. Then King Leopold persuaded a number of European powers to recognize his personal authority over the Congo.

At the same time Germany, which had sent many missionaries and explorers to Africa but had played a minor commercial role there, annexed South-West Africa, Togoland, the Cameroons, Tanganyika, and Ruanda-Urundi. The scramble for Africa had begun.

In December 1884 all the European powers with interests in Africa met at a conference in Berlin, Germany. They came to discuss slavery, the rights of Africans, Leopold's seizure of the Congo, Germany's annexations, and African trade matters. They divided much of coastal Africa into European spheres of influence and made vague agreements about the rules that should govern future annexations. If the major European powers had needed any further stimulus to move in Africa, it was provided at the Berlin conference.

By 1890 the coastal regions of Africa were marked off into territories under the control of Belgium, Great Britain, France, Germany, Italy, Portugal, and Spain. Inland the borders of the European claims often faded out where the countryside was poorly known or where an African state was still in control of an area. But by 1910 these territorial lines were fairly precise.

France, at the time of the Berlin conference, was established in various parts of northern Africa, around the Senegal River, and in the Gabon region. It then moved quickly southward into the Sahara, pressed up the Senegal and then eastward along the Niger River, and pushed northward from the Gabon coast. French forces met opposition from the still active Sudanic states; but now they were determined. By 1910 France had crushed most of the opposition, and laid claim to a vast area of Saharan and Sudanic lands that included the area comprising modern Algeria, Morocco, and Tunisia, in North Africa; Mauritania, Senegal, Guinea, Mali, Upper Volta, Ivory Coast, Benin, Togo, and Niger, in West Africa; and Chad, Central African Empire, Cameroon, Gabon, and Congo (Brazzaville), in Central Africa. France had lost out in Northeast Africa, except for the small enclave of French Somaliland; but it held undisputed claim to the huge island of Madagascar.

Great Britain, already established on the coasts of

Gambia, Sierra Leone, the Gold Coast, and Nigeria, limited its efforts in western Africa to extending British authority inland in these territories. Like France, it met stiff opposition from such strong African states as Ashanti and Hausaland; but the better-equipped and better-organized British forces won out.

It was in the southern and eastern parts of Africa that the great British effort was made. Goading the Boers of Southern Africa into war in 1899, the British defeated them in 1902 and joined the Boer and British territories to form the Union of South Africa. Britain set up protectorates over Bechuanaland, Basutoland, and Swaziland and enforced British sovereignty northward in Rhodesia and Nyasaland. In eastern Africa, blocked by the German annexation of Tanganyika, Britain moved inland from the city of Mombasa and also southward down the Nile to gain control over Kenya, Uganda, Sudan, and the northern part of what is present-day Somalia.

Germany had made its bid for land in Africa about the time of the Berlin conference, and contented itself with subduing the peoples of its territories—Togoland, the Cameroons, South-West Africa, Tanganyika, and Ruanda-Urundi.

Portugal's historic footholds in Portuguese Guinea, Angola, and Mozambique stayed more or less intact, but it made increasing efforts in the interior to ensure its power.

Strong criticism from many European governments and the United States forced Belgium to acquire from its king, Leopold, the vast Congo empire that he had assembled as his personal possession, when it became clear that he was ruthlessly exploiting and killing countless thousands of the Congolese people.

Spain emerged from the scramble with several small

territories that other powers considered hardly worth contesting: Ifni, Spanish Morocco, Spanish Sahara, and Rio Muni.

Italy's African holdings were notably insecure. It enforced its authority in southern Somaliland and Libya but was beaten back from central Ethiopia by Emperor Menelik. Although Italy held Eritrea on the coast, it had to admit defeat in Ethiopia until the 1930's.

By 1910 there were only two African countries undisputedly in the hands of Africans: Ethiopia and Liberia. The Union of South Africa, an independent member of the British Commonwealth, was ruled by its British and Boer settlers. The rest of Africa had passed from African rule in 1870 to European control by 1910. European partitioning was accomplished; and fifty years of colonial rule began.

◀ 6 ▶

Independence: The Giant Stirs

The rapid colonial conquest of Africa between 1880 and 1910 succeeded partly through superior European force and partly because some Africans did not fully understand what was happening until it was too late. Before 1880 the European colonial territories along the coast of western Africa were small, and relatively harmless from the African point of view. The colonial governors ruled with a benevolent hand, by and large, and the peoples under them were comparatively prosperous and secure. Colonial commerce with free Africans was peaceful and conducted on equal terms.

It did not seem menacing, therefore, when the colonial authorities in the 1880's and 1890's prepared treaties that offered their protection to African kings and emirs. Some, such as the leaders of the Ashanti and the Fulani, resisted and fought; but others signed the treaties, not realizing what they implied, and did not at first resist the colonial representatives and their armed escorts. By the time the Africans realized that the treaties meant subjection, the well-armed colonial forces were in control, and protest was futile.

Where Africans did protest European incursions, the result was often horrible. Many hundreds were killed in the Ashanti wars; but hundreds of thousands—possibly millions—were slaughtered in the Congo by King Leopold's forces. In the Maji-Maji rebellion in Tanganyika, during the years 1905 through 1907, the toll of those killed or starved was 120,000. Whole tribal areas were devastated in the Cameroons during the rebellions of 1904 and 1905, and in South-West Africa during the Herero wars of 1904.

The same pattern appeared in Southern Africa, where white men were settling in large numbers. A succession of ten Xhosa wars had begun in 1790 and lasted until 1890, when white power made further wars futile. The Zulu wars, though briefer, were equally bloody. The Basuto people battled the Boers for years, and the Matebele people rebelled a number of times against the British. Although many of these African protests were quickly and ruthlessly suppressed, they all reflected an African resentment of European control that colonialism never really killed.

During the period when colonial control was consolidated—from about 1890 to 1950—Africans were prevented from expressing their resentment of domination. Open opposition was futile, and the systems of colonial government provided no democratic mechanism for expressions of the desire for change.

Yet Africa was more restless during this period than the case appeared on the surface. Perhaps the chief expression of dissatisfaction was through religion, especially in the Christianized areas. More and more African religious sects split off from the established churches. In these new separatist churches the African was likened to the Old Testament Jew, and the white man to the Egyptian conquerors of the Jews.

Occasionally the churches preached open rebellion against the oppressor. In such cases the colonial authorities took swift and forceful action: the church was closed, and its leaders were exiled, jailed, or even executed. But the colonial governments, representing Christian countries, could not abolish all churches. And so the African church helped to keep resistance alive.

At the same time, the schools established by white Christian missionaries were educating Africans. These schools were relatively few, but potentially of great significance to Africa. For it was the educated African, rather than the traditional kings and chiefs, who would eventually voice the yearnings of Africa's people for freedom.

The mission schools did not teach rebellion, but the African pupils who read the thoughts of Europe's great philosophers—Rousseau, Locke, Hume, Dante—were inspired by their ideas of liberty, which contrasted strongly with the reality of colonial domination. These students read, too, of the great American advocates of democracy, such as Jefferson and Lincoln, and of the search of America's blacks for freedom and equal rights.

Despite the chasm that has separated Afro-Americans from their African cousins for many generations, each group has played a vital role in the emancipation of the other during the twentieth century. The ideas and personalities of modern African nationalism were deeply influenced by those of the early American civil rights movement, and especially by W. E. B. Du Bois, a founder of the National Association for the Advancement of Colored People.

By the end of World War I virtually all African traditional chiefs and kings had been subjugated. However, a handful of African teachers, ministers, doctors, and lawyers had appeared in the more advanced areas. The countries of Senegal, Gambia, Sierra Leone, Ivory Coast, Gold Coast, and Nigeria all had their "new African" spokesmen, and were developing educational systems that reached more and more people. These spokesmen could not play active, militant political roles; but they did form discussion groups, clubs, literary societies, alumni associations—and, eventually, more ambitious organizations that had a quietly nationalistic political complexion, such as the Aborigines' Rights Protective Association in the Gold Coast and the Nigerian National Democratic Party. These associations were to argue for the rights of African chiefs, civil servants, and professional men; to present the views of African leaders to the colonial governments; and to discuss matters affecting the territories' welfare.

Another change in Africa during the first decades of this century was the movement of many people to the cities, resulting in the gradual formation of an urban, laboring African population. These people were in touch with the ideas, the products, and the forces of the modern world outside Africa, and were consequently very conscious of the fact that in the twentieth century Africa was being left behind.

World War II was an upheaval that dramatically changed the world—and Africa. France and Great Britain, the two major colonial powers, depended on Africa and its peoples during World War II. When Charles de Gaulle decided to fight on for France even after its defeat, his first base of support was French Equatorial Africa—whose governor, Félix Eboué, supported de Gaulle and supplied him with troops. African troops from both British and French territories fought for the Western Allies, and military bases in western Africa were vital to the Allied cause. When the war ended, both Britain and France found it difficult to forget the debt they owed for African support during the darkest days.

The Africans who joined the armed forces for service in Europe, Asia, and North Africa acquired a knowledge of the rest of the world, and a sense of their own place in it, that made it impossible for them to settle back quietly into colonial subjugation. They had fought together with white soldiers on terms of comparative equality, and they had seen white people at home, as ordinary people—very different from the lofty colonial officials of Africa.

When the thousands of African servicemen returned after the war, they added a new element to the stirring populations. The people on the home front had been touched by the war too. They had seen thousands of white soldiers who were common men, like themselves. They had been urged by the officials of Britain and France to support the war effort, and they had a new sense of their own value in relation to Europe.

But the chief role in the formation of the African nationalist movement was to be played by a small group of African students educated in Europe and America. Some of these students went abroad for higher education just before the war, and returned home in the late 1940's. Others went abroad after the war, returning to Africa in the early 1950's. As they returned home, they lighted the spark that moved Africa from colonialism to freedom.

One of the first of these new leaders was Dr. Nnamdi Azikiwe, a Nigerian who had studied at Lincoln University and Howard University in the United States and had returned to Nigeria before World War II. He started an outspokenly nationalist newspaper, helped to form the first openly political Nigerian nationalist movement, and inspired hundreds of young people in Nigeria, the Gold Coast, and Sierra Leone to follow in his footsteps.

One young man inspired by Azikiwe became one of the most prominent nationalist leaders: Kwame Nkrumah of Ghana. Nkrumah followed Azikiwe to America. He studied at Lincoln University and the University of Pennsylvania—like Azikiwe, working his way through college. He, too, was excited by the opportunities for individual development in America, but was angered by racial discrimination and the fact that his native Africa was derided as savage and primitive by most of the people he met. Like hundreds of other young Africans studying abroad, he developed a burning ambition to free Africa and lead it back to a position of dignity and respect in the world.

KWAME NKRUMAH
OF GHANA

While in America, Nkrumah read the works of W. E. B. Du Bois and came to know this great black leader. He was deeply impressed by Du Bois and his zeal for advancement of blacks. The two men developed a strong friendship that eventually influenced Du Bois to become a Ghanaian citizen and to spend his last years of life in Ghana.

Nkrumah went on to further study in England, and in 1945 helped Du Bois convene a Pan-Africanist Congress there. It was the fifth of these meetings that Du Bois had organized—but the first that had substantial participation by Africans. The first four congresses had been held in 1919, 1921, 1923, and 1927. They brought together Africans, American blacks, West Indians, and black intellectuals from France and England. They emphasized ways to advance the position of blacks and Africans in general, rather than ways in which Africa could be freed of colonialism.

But the Fifth Pan-Africanist Congress was different. The personalities present had in many cases known each other for years and had influenced each other greatly. There were students and ex-students from many parts of Africa, intellectuals and writers from Africa and the Americas, trade-union leaders, poets, and professional men. They focused their attention on Africa in a serious way, condemning the policies of the colonial powers and calling for reforms and advancement on a broad front. Many of the Africans present went on to hold high positions in their countries after independence; and two of them—Kwame Nkrumah and Jomo Kenyatta—eventually became presidents of African nations.

Nkrumah returned to the Gold Coast in 1947 to become secretary of the United Gold Coast Convention, which was the first genuinely political movement in that country since the colonial conquest. The UGCC was led by older men—lawyers, doctors, civil servants, chiefs, teachers—with the participation of a few of the younger, more militant ex-students from abroad. In less than a year Nkrumah broke away from the UGCC to form the Convention People's Party, appealing to the workers, farmers, students, unemployed, and urban people. The CPP quickly developed broad support, swept into power when the first elections were held in 1951, and led the Gold Coast to freedom in 1957 as the new nation of Ghana.

Nationalist movements similar to Ghana's Convention People's Party were rapidly gathering power in western Africa, and in some other parts of the continent, between 1947 and 1955. In territory after territory the story was the same. Militant young students, fired with zeal for Africa's freedom, returned from abroad and began to preach freedom to the people. Their message was first heard, and accepted, by the townsfolk—the detribalized Africans. The chiefs and the older educated Africans, grown timid and conservative under decades of colonial regulation, sometimes opposed the new movements; but the younger people of the countryside tended to follow their urban fellows.

African nationalism spread so quickly and so widely that its leaders received overwhelming support as soon as the colonial governments permitted elections. A favorable vote from over 90 percent of the electorate—often voting for the first time—was not uncommon.

The message of the nationalists was relatively uncomplicated. They proclaimed that Africa must be free; that colonialism was immoral and oppressive; that Africans must decide their own destinies, must hold up their heads as free men in the world community, and must achieve the progress that the rest of the world was achieving but that colonialism had denied to Africa.

Underlying the nationalist message were anger and shame at Africa's subject condition, at its backwardness and poverty. And there was the deep resentment that had its roots in the colonial conquest of fifty years before. The nationalists urged the people of Africa to restore their former position of freedom and consequence, to return to the greatness that colonialism had suppressed.

Another part of the nationalist ideology was pan-Africanism: the belief that all Africans have basic similarities and ought to show a kindred, united front to the world. The Africans who preached nationalism had for years associated together as students in foreign lands. They recognized in one another both a deep, underlying resentment of colonialism and a new hope for Africa. To them Africa was the important thing— not the tribe, not the clan, not the artificially created colonial territory. It seemed only natural that all Africa should be free and united against a world that, so they believed, had conspired to exclude them from the dynamic events of the twentieth century. Pan-Africanism was to meet obstacles after independence had been won; but in the early days of African nationalism it had a magnetic appeal.

The growth of the nationalist movement in the Gold Coast was paralleled in much of West Africa. It took a slightly different form in each territory because of local personalities, conditions, and history.

In the French territories the African intellectuals had traditional ties with sympathetic forces in France itself, where there was a vigorous equalitarian frame of mind in the labor movement and in the Communist party. The Africans who studied in France went back to Africa to organize their people with the help of these French forces. For some years these former students were more interested in a greater role for Africa in French affairs than they were in African independence.

This argument was aided by the organization of the

French Community. This arrangement allowed the overseas territories of France to share with France itself a voice in their common destiny. Under the provisions of the Community, African territories elected delegates to the National Assembly in France. When elections were held, the African nationalist leaders found themselves in the position of campaigning for seats in Paris. It was not until 1958, when France adopted a new constitution allowing limited self-government in Africa, that the French African nationalists began to think of independence as a serious alternative to a larger voice in French affairs.

The Portuguese and Belgian territories of Africa lagged behind British and French Africa in the development of the postwar nationalist movement, for three reasons. First, the colonial authorities suppressed any expression of nationalist sentiment; the Portuguese continued to do so with ruthless energy until defeated by African freedom fighters in 1974. Second, these territories were less advanced in educational opportunities for the people. They did not have a class of foreign-educated leaders that could effectively organize the nationalist forces. And third, Portugal and Belgium were not affected by the war in quite the same way as Britain and France—nor were their African territories. Belgium was defeated and occupied by the Germans, and was never able to develop a force comparable to the Free French under de Gaulle. Portugal, as a neutral dictatorship, was not swept by the anticolonial, anti-imperialist feelings that appeared elsewhere. But nationalism later came even to these African territories. Belgium's three dependencies eventually obtained independence; and in Portugal's territories guerrilla warfare finally led to freedom.

Such great powers as the United States, the Soviet

Union, and China, professing a moral commitment to self-determination for colonial peoples after World War II, responded with some sympathy to the emerging nationalist movements. The United Nations charter, to which many of the colonial powers were signatories, contained anticolonial declarations. In the United Nations the new African nationalists had a forum in which to voice their appeals for freedom. Great Britain and France, even if inclined to cling to their colonial empires, faced stiff opposition from most of the world.

Also, after the war the strength of colonialism had been drained away. In both Great Britain and France important segments of public opinion were opposed to continuing a colonial empire. Both countries faced grievous problems of reconstruction at home after the devastation of the war. They had to devote their energies to this task, rather than to maintaining an unpopular and increasingly shaky colonial system.

With many new African nations now in existence, it is apparent, looking back to the 1945–1960 era, that colonialism in Africa was doomed. But at the time it was not so apparent. The African nationalist movements then seemed fragile, and many observers regarded African spokesmen as dreamers, not as realistic leaders.

Also, the determination of the colonial powers seemed stronger than it actually was. In the first few years of African nationalism many of the African leaders felt that they faced a long, difficult battle for freedom. They were surprised when the struggle proved to be brief and peaceful.

The forces of nationalism were strong; the climate of world opinion was favorable; and the will of the colonial powers to resist was weak. And so independence came —first to a few, then to the many.

In 1950 all Africa was under the yoke of colonialism, with the exceptions of Liberia, Ethiopia, Egypt—and South Africa, where the white settler was free but the indigenous African totally subjugated.

In 1951, almost by chance, Libya became independent. A former Italian colony, Libya became a United Nations trust territory after World War II. The United States and other Western powers, fearful of Soviet involvement in Libya while it was administered by the United Nations, arranged for it to become independent —almost before it was ready.

In 1956 Morocco and Tunisia became independent of France. Both countries had been true nations for centuries; they were under French protection rather than being full colonies. Sudan then became the first British dependency in Africa to achieve independence, in 1956.

Ghana became independent in 1957; and Guinea followed suit a year later, as the first true colony of France to break with the mother country. Nigeria, which might have gained independence sooner but for its complicated internal federal situation, became fully independent of Britain in 1960.

Before 1960 there were ten independent nations in Africa. But during a single year, 1960, seventeen nations, including almost all the French territories, became free. Since 1960 more than a dozen others have joined their ranks.

Roughly 5 percent of Africa's people still live under alien rule. Virtually all of these are under white control in the Republic of South Africa, Namibia, and Zimbabwe. Africans in the latter two countries are making progress in their struggle for freedom, and will become free soon. Only in South Africa does it appear that alien rule can hold out a few more years against African pro-

SP. MOROCCO

FR. MOROCCO

TUNISIA
(French)

Mediterranean Sea

AFRICA—1945

RIO DE ORO
(Spanish)

ALGERIA
(French)

LIBYA
(Italian)

EGYPT

FRENCH WEST AFRICA

ANGLO
EGYPTIAN
SUDAN

ERITREA
(Italian)

FRENCH
SOMALILAND

GAMBIA
(British)

PORT.
GUINEA

GOLD COAST
(British)

NIGERIA
(British)

FRENCH EQUAT. AFRICA

ETHIOPIA

BRITISH
SOMALILAND

SIERRA
LEONE
(British)

LIBERIA

UGANDA
(Br.)

BR. TOGOLAND

FR. TOGOLAND

BR. CAMEROONS

FR. CAMEROUN

Atlantic Ocean

BELGIAN
CONGO

KENYA
(British)

ITALIAN
SOMALI-
LAND

RUANDA
URUNDI
(Belgian)

TANGANYIKA
(British)

*Indian
Ocean*

RIO MUNI
(Sp.)

CABINDA
(Port.)

ANGOLA
(Port.)

N. RHODESIA
(Br.)

NYASALAND
(British)

MOZAMBIQUE
(Portuguese)

SOUTHERN RHODESIA
(British)

BECHUANALAND
(British)

MADAGASCAR
(French)

SOUTH-WEST
AFRICA
(Union of South Africa)

SWAZILAND
(British)

UNION OF SOUTH AFRICA

BASUTOLAND
(British)

Jefferson

AFRICA—1962

MOROCCO
TUNISIA
Mediterranean Sea
ALGERIA
LIBYA
U.A.R.
EGYPT
SPANISH
SAHARA
MAURITANIA
MALI
NIGER
CHAD
SUDAN
FRENCH
SOMALILAND
ETHIOPIA
SOMALIA
SENEGAL
GAMBIA
PORT.
GUINEA
UPPER
VOLTA
GUINEA
NIGERIA
SIERRA LEONE
IVORY
COAST
GHANA
CENTRAL
AFRICAN
REPUBLIC
LIBERIA
CAMEROON
UGANDA
KENYA
TOGO
DAHOMEY
SPANISH
GUINEA
GABON
REPUBLIC OF
THE CONGO
RWANDA
BURUNDI
Atlantic Ocean
CONGO REPUBLIC
TANGANYIKA
(British)
ZANZIBAR
Indian
Ocean
NYASALAND
ANGOLA
(Port.)
N. RHODESIA
(British)
MOZAMBIQUE
(Portuguese)
SOUTH-WEST
AFRICA
(Union of South Africa)
SOUTHERN
RHODESIA
(British)
MALAGASY
REPUBLIC
BECHUANALAND
(British)
SWAZILAND
SOUTH AFRICA
BASUTOLAND
(British)
Jefferson

Became independent before 1945

Became independent since 1945

Non-independent

132 / UNDERSTANDING AFRICA

test, and eventually Africans will gain power even in that last foothold of European reign.

Thus, for the most part, Africans face the future as citizens of independent African nations, ruled by leaders from their own ranks. But the search has not yet ended. The people of southern Africa face a troubled future, which may take many painful years to unfold.

◄ 7 ►

Africa's Search for Prosperity

The pattern of colonial economic exploitation was roughly the same in all the colonial territories. By 1880, the slave trade ended. The trade in Africa's indigenous products was not large enough to be important to a wealthy, industrialized Europe. To take advantage of its African empire, each European power, together with the great commercial interests of Europe, wanted to find new sources of wealth there.

Generally the European interests concentrated on agricultural and forest products, which required little investment; and on mineral products, which promised high returns on investments. In the forest areas of West Africa, oil palms were one of the first attractions. Africans could be induced to harvest the oil-rich nuts from trees that grew wild. The nuts were then pressed to produce vegetable oil for Europe's soaps and chemical needs.

In the same forest areas, cocoa also proved an easy and profitable crop. Like oil palms, cacao trees could be grown and harvested by Africans, then the cocoa sold by Europeans with little investment. In later years rubber, which required more investment and organization, became a major product. Along the eastern and western coastal fringes of Africa coconut palms, used for oil and copra, became a key product.

Farther inland, especially in the Sudan region of western Africa, peanuts provided the answer. Well adapted for growth in the savannah soils and climate, and valued in Europe for its excellent oil, the peanut could be grown and harvested by Africans with minimal machinery and wage outlay.

Africa had long been famous for gold, diamonds, and copper. Later, other minerals were found and exploited.

In both mineral exploitation and crop production, the basic principle was the same: invest only enough to ensure a profit, pay Africans the minimum prices or wages, and expropriate the proceeds to Europe. Neither the colonial governments nor the commercial interests gave serious consideration to the development of Africa's wealth for Africans.

Yet Africans derived some benefits. As time went on, the more enlightened colonial governments used some of the money for Africa's development. Roads and railroads were built. Schools, operated and supported by missionaries, were encouraged by colonial governments. Cities were expanded and modernized. Harbors were dredged, and port facilities were constructed.

PALM KERNELS

Hospitals and health services were established. Gradually research stations were developed to study insect pests, crop diseases, animal husbandry, and plant improvement.

When colonialism ended, it bequeathed a thin network of roads and railroads; a few modern ports and airports; schools and systems of formal education; a skeletal health service; some research stations and pilot projects in agriculture, fish stocking, forestry, and animal husbandry; a pattern of cash crop and mineral production; modernized cities; and a people hungry to move upward to greater prosperity.

The new governments of Africa's independent nations resolved that Africa's wealth would forevermore remain in Africa. They associated European colonialism with European commercial exploitation; and, once free of colonialism, they still held a deep suspicion of capitalism.

The avowed economic policy of most new African governments was socialism. They could not accept the implications of socialism as it is defined in the Soviet Union and Eastern Europe, but they believed that only under the control of the national government could the wealth of Africa be exploited for Africans.

Many of Africa's new leaders saw that neither their governments nor their people possessed the capital and skills needed for economic growth. In most cases, though they stressed state control and planning of economic development, they still welcomed foreign private investment. Regulations were quickly established to prevent exploitation by private capital, but nowhere in Africa was private investment prohibited. Even in those African states that have been the most vigorous advocates of socialist philosophy, there has been a modicum of private investment from abroad. Africa's new nations

AFRICA'S MAJOR PRODUCTS

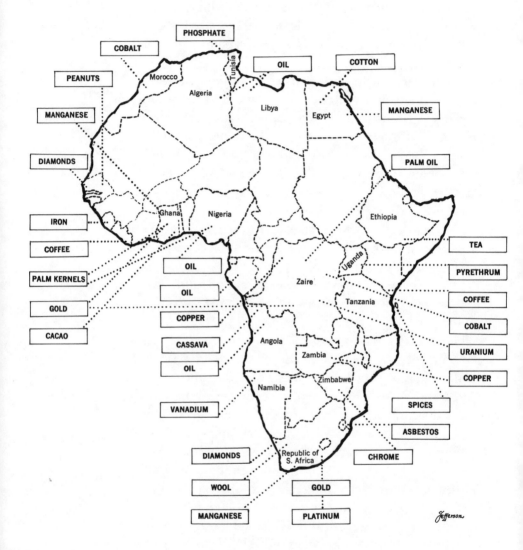

had to accept realistically the fact that they needed assistance from all possible quarters—even from the foreign capitalism that they knew had historically exploited Africa. Most new African nations, however, have concentrated on economic developments that the state could undertake with the aid of grants or loans from abroad, or through its own resources, before looking to private investment, whether foreign or domestic.

In every new African nation education has been given precedence, partly because the people demand education for their children and partly because the leaders know that education is a prerequisite for economic development.

Industrialization is also very high on the priority list. Conscious of their peoples' rural, agricultural, simple way of life, African leaders have tended to look on the development of industry as the most effective—and visible—means of gaining the twentieth-century prosperity they seek. Mining also is regarded as a ready means of economic development, and most nations have eagerly encouraged mineral surveys and investments in mining enterprises.

The development of the cities has received a great deal of attention. After centuries of isolation and "backwardness," African leaders want to see a shining demonstration of contemporary success: tall, modern buildings; paved roads; luxury hotels; and impressive monuments.

Regrettably, most African nations have placed a higher value on these sectors than on agriculture and rural development. As a result, much of the prosperity achieved since independence is limited to the few large cities, while the great majority of the people in the rural areas have had little change in their lives. In the years since the nationalist movement became a dynamic force, Africa's leaders have had time to develop their impressive political capacities—but little else. At the time of independence they had little experience in running large governments, in analyzing basic economic problems, or in planning sound national development.

Many African leaders complain, with good reason, that their efforts to develop their countries are impeded by European "neocolonialism," which is economic control maintained after political rule has ended. Great American and European firms set most of the prices for African products and for European manufactured goods, and these firms or Western governments possess most of the capital that is needed to finance African development. There is much evidence that the West thus allows Africa to develop only at a slow pace, and that many African leaders receive wealth and Western support for not protesting Western economic control.

Africa's first years of independence have brought the rapid realization to its leaders that independence, in and of itself, cannot solve their problems. Independence has only brought Africans into direct confronta-

tion with their difficulties. If Africa were content with a return to the ways of life of the past century, its problems would be less complex. But Africa has embarked on a course of great transformation into the modern age; and the problems it faces are manifold.

Perhaps Africa's first obstacle has been a dearth of skills. In many of the new nations, when independence came, there were only a few dozen college graduates, a few hundred secondary-school graduates, and a few thousand people who had had some primary-school education. The vast majority of the people were illiterate and were skilled only in the ways of simple peasantry. To build a prosperous nation from an underdeveloped country requires skilled administrators, engineers, doctors, teachers, agriculturalists, mechanics, electricians, and artisans. But from the highest levels of leadership down to the common citizen, many African states started with only a handful of educated and experienced people.

The solution in each country has been roughly the same: education has been expanded at an almost breakneck pace. In the meantime experts must be borrowed from the former colonial power, from the United States, from the Soviet Union, from the United Nations —from all over the world. Every new nation in Africa has gone through a period of depending on foreign skills while it trains its own people, and not even the most advanced has yet been able to dispense completely with experts from abroad.

An equally critical obstacle in the search for prosperity has been the lack of money and capital. All new African nations have had to depend heavily on loans, investments, and grants-in-aid from abroad. And new capital from abroad has been difficult to attract except where it would bring large profits to the foreign investor.

During the early 1960's there was enough Cold War spirit to create an air of competition between East and West in aiding the new African nations. The United States and the Soviet Union, especially, each extended aid to ensure that the other did not gain the advantage in Africa. Later, however, the competition quieted, and the flow of aid to Africa has declined steadily since the late 1960's.

Investment is naturally attracted where risks are small and potential profits reasonably large. Where these conditions are met, investors have shown interest: bauxite in Ghana and Guinea, iron in Liberia, oil in Nigeria, automobile assembly in Zimbabwe. But the capital needs of Africa's new nations are often for different kinds of development, where profits may be years in coming: better transport, mineral exploration, soil surveys, agricultural experiments.

Conditions in Africa have often discouraged investors, both governmental and private, who might otherwise have been interested. Most notably the instability of Africa's new governments has dampened the enthusiasm of potential investors. When radical changes occur in governments or where there is evidence of civil unrest, investors become wary.

Even where stability prevails and profits seem potentially good, there have been other obstacles to the flow of capital that Africa needs. Poor communications and transportation are major ones. The country of Niger, for example, has discovered important deposits of uranium and several other minerals. But Niger's roads are poor; it has no railroad; and it is hundreds of miles inland. The sheer difficulty and cost of moving mine products to the sea are serious deterrents to investment in the mining of Niger's ores. An enormous initial investment would be needed before any profits could be realized.

For other kinds of investments, such as in manufacturing, Africa's markets are frequently limited. In many nations the population is too small and too poor to buy enough goods so as to attract investors for manufacture of the goods there.

Another serious problem lies in the area of agriculture. Too little research has been done to find new and more valuable crops. Soils have not been adequately analyzed. Insects and diseases that threaten crops and livestock are not yet conquered, either from lack of funds to take effective measures or because effective measures have not yet been discovered.

In farming techniques and attitudes, problems abound. Wasteful ways of using land are still followed, exhausting soils that were not rich to begin with. Farmers in Africa (like farmers the world over) are slow to adopt new methods and new crops. Many sound basic agricultural practices, such as using crop by-products to feed animals and using animal fertilizer to enrich the soil, are not yet in widespread use. Although the density of population in Africa is generally low, Africa suffers the same effects of "population explosion" as other underdeveloped lands. The birth rate is high, and the

death rate is decreasing. The pressure of population in the small fertile areas is increasing. And, although the available land outside these areas is ample, it is capable of supporting only sparse populations.

In the process of facing up to its real problems, Africa has not been idle. In most countries progress has been achieved. The income earned by the average worker is slowly rising, although it can barely keep ahead of the rapid increase in population. Several countries, however, have been able to increase the value of the goods they produce by between 5 and 10 percent each year. Ghana, Ivory Coast, and Liberia, in terms of the rising value of what they produce annually, have been among the more rapidly developing countries in the world.

Most African nations have concentrated on the building up of "infrastructure," or the facilities that are prerequisite for development: transportation, communication, civic organization, education, and health and welfare services.

In all the new nations, main roads and rural "feeder" roads have been extended in the past few years. Many roads that were once usable only in good weather have been improved so that they can be used under all weather conditions. Between large cities and between coastal cities and the interior, many major highways have been paved.

Railroads have been extended in several African countries, bringing cheap transportation to underdeveloped areas that once were isolated. Railroad cars are being replaced with more modern equipment, and diesel locomotives are replacing steam. Bridges have been built to span large rivers, replacing the antiquated ferries that had previously been the only means of crossing.

Every African country with a seacoast has made great

efforts to establish or improve port facilities. From Mauritania on the Atlantic to Somalia on the Indian Ocean coast, new ports, jetties, warehouses, and cargo-handling installations have appeared, and old harbors have been deepened.

In almost every African capital, airports have been improved, runways lengthened to accommodate modern jets, and new passenger and cargo terminals constructed. New aircraft have been added; new routes connecting African cities with other parts of the world have been established; and internal air services in most countries have been increased.

Africa's new nations are trying to better communication between the hinterland and the main cities by enlarging postal, telephone, and telegraph facilities, and developing radio and television broadcasting. Radio broadcasting, because it reaches large numbers of people over great distances, receives special attention—even though broadcasts may have to be repeated on the same station in several different languages. Radio programs devote much of their time to news of government activities.

In addition, nation after nation has experimented with new ministries and governmental departments devoted to the planning and supervision of national development. Foreign experts have been asked to study conditions and to recommend more effective governmental institutions to serve the country's needs.

A number of African countries have undertaken manpower studies in order to predict their needs for trained people in future years. In these studies, careful estimates are made of the number of skilled jobs that will have to be filled each successive year. Then the number of students finishing school in various fields of study is projected and matched against the job predictions.

Until independence came, the majority of African children had no schools to attend, no matter how eagerly they wanted education. Since independence African leaders have felt that their first task should be the rapid expansion of the schools. Primary schools and secondary schools, especially, have been doubled, trebled, quadrupled in number.

Health and welfare services also have been expanded. African governments have tried to build new hospitals and dispensaries, recruit more doctors, and increase public health measures. Much remains to be done in this area. There are few African doctors, and foreign doctors are expensive and hard to recruit. But the drive for better health services has begun.

These efforts of African governments have produced progress in most fields. The least show of progress is in rural living conditions and in agriculture. Cash crops have, since independence, been the chief underpinning of the African economies—but at the same time a source of great uncertainty. Where agricultural development has occurred, it has often been in the form of expanding production of the one or two cash crops upon which the country depends. For example, if a country gains most of its income from coffee sales, it has typically urged more farmers to grow more coffee. The result has been an increase in the supply of such a product—and a corresponding decline in world prices. Realizing the unprofitable outcome of this kind of crop expansion, African governments are now beginning to encourage farmers to plant new cash crops in large worldwide demand. Less attention has been paid, however, to crops that will provide farmers with more and better foods, or that will sell profitably on the domestic market.

Also, Africa's leaders have for years looked hopefully

COFFEE

to mineral production as a source of prosperity; but the lack of sound geological surveys, the difficulties in exploring for minerals, and poor transportation facilities have hindered progress. Despite these obstacles, however, African governments are according it highest priority.

In recent years rich mineral deposits have been discovered in Africa, often near enough to waterpower or coal sources to encourage investors to exploit them. Iron has become a major factor in Liberia's increasing prosperity. Bauxite is becoming a key resource in Ghana and Guinea, now that dams built in both countries are able to produce inexpensive electricity. Botswana has discovered important copper deposits, which are now being mined. Nigeria has become, in the past few years, one of the largest oil-producing countries in the world. The Sahara also is potentially a rich source of oil.

As each year passes, Africa discovers new minerals and opens bidding to foreign investors for their exploration and production. Where the investments have been secured, the African governments have tried to negotiate agreements that guarantee a reasonable share of the profits. This profit sharing is a source of new income for the governments, which in turn use it to expand education, research, transportation facilities, and public services.

For the foreseeable future, Africa will have to earn most of the money it needs from its mineral reserves, its cash crops, and other product assets such as lumber and fish. It is unlikely that Africa's position as a producer of raw materials and a purchaser of foreign manufactured goods can be changed fundamentally for many decades. But some changes can be made: Africa can process more of its own foodstuffs and can manufacture certain consumer goods that were formerly obtained from abroad.

Paradoxically, Africa's commerce has been so confined to the export of raw materials that it sends some goods to Europe and then buys them back after they have been processed there. Ghana, the world's chief exporter of cocoa beans, until recently bought its refined cocoa and chocolate from Europe. Several Central African countries sell tobacco abroad to Europe, then buy the cigarettes from Europe, made of their own tobacco. Western Africa's coastal peoples, great fishermen, also purchase canned fish from abroad.

In the same vein, many African countries that depend on the sale of certain cash crops abroad have used part of their income from those crops to buy other foods from abroad. Their farmers are so occupied with producing cocoa, peanuts, oil palms, or rubber that they are not able to grow rice, wheat, millet, or livestock, and instead buy some of these necessities from Europe.

Recognizing the inefficiency and high costs of this pattern, independent Africa seeks ways to change it. Gradually canneries and food-freezing plants are appearing. They buy meats, fish, and vegetables in one part of the country to sell them to other parts of the same country. Cement factories have been built in many African countries to produce it from local materials, whereas previously cement had been imported.

In some countries textile mills have been established, to manufacture from African cotton the cloth that Africa has for years bought from Europe, India, China, Japan, and the United States. Plywood factories now make plywood from African lumber, instead of shipping raw timber abroad and then using the proceeds to buy foreign plywood. Most African countries have developed cigarette factories, breweries, match factories, and joineries to produce, for local consumption, other products that once had to be imported.

As some of the African countries—nations such as Kenya, Zambia, Ghana, Nigeria, and Ivory Coast—become more prosperous, they are able to attract heavier industries: automobile-assembly plants, bicycle-manufacturing plants, radio-assembly plants, metal-fabricating plants, and plastics factories. In these industries, raw materials or manufactured parts are purchased from abroad, then put together for local sale as finished products.

Each time a new industry of this type begins, on a small scale, it represents a step forward in Africa's search for prosperity. More Africans become employed in the cash economy; prices to the consumer tend to be lower; and more of the profits of the manufacturer remain in Africa.

A visitor returning to Africa after a long absence is struck by the visible evidence of economic development and greater prosperity. New modern buildings, better-paved roads, more cars on the roads, new schools, and better-dressed people can be seen in the major cities. National budgets have grown; literacy has increased;

health has been improved. Yet in many of the new nations the statistics are not impressive. The eradication of some formerly serious diseases and the reduction in infant mortality, combined with a high birthrate, give Africa a rapidly increasing population. As wealth increases, so does the number of people among whom it must be shared.

The fact is that some Africans are moving toward prosperity—but most Africans are not. In the countryside life continues as it always has: a constant daily round of work to produce enough for a meager living, but no more. There is a tendency to concentrate development in the cities and in easily accessible areas of the country. Not enough progress has yet spread to the rural areas; and this leads to unrest as these areas begin to resent the growing gap between themselves and the cities.

But there are ample grounds for hope. Much progress has been made in improving Africa's transportation, communications, and public services. Both mineral and agricultural potentials exist that have not yet been tapped. And most important of all, Africa's leaders and educated men are facing, with increasing realism, the problems that lie before them.

◀ 8 ▶

Building African Nations

The African states that are now independent are very different one from another. Some are small in area, some large. Some are very heavily populated; some have scant populations. Some are potentially wealthy, some desperately poor. Some are clearly nations, with their people fully united and conscious of their common nationhood; others call themselves nations, but are engaged in a difficult struggle to unite quite diverse peoples into a spirit of genuine unity.

Since 1960 these new states have been referred to universally as "the new nations of Africa." But are they true nations? In normal usage, a nation is a large group of people, sharing the same territory, speaking the same language, cherishing the same traditions, bound by a common government, and conscious of themselves as one people. In some of the new states of Africa, however, it is rare to find all these attributes present within the same state. In many of them, in fact, there are several different groups of people (erroneously referred to as "tribes"), each of which could actually fit the definition of a "nation," except for sharing a common government.

Colonial history has thrown these ethnic groups together in new and independent political states. In this and many other ways they have been confronted with a life situation and a civil framework that virtually demand that they think of themselves as nations rather than ethnic groups. The modern world looks on the peoples of Ghana—whether they be Ewe, Fanti, or Ashanti—as Ghanaians. And the peoples of Ghana, eager to be a part of world affairs, have very quickly learned to think of themselves as Ghanaians, although they are still very conscious of their ethnic origins. This development of a new self-image of nationhood by millions of Africans is not very different, except for its rapidity, from what has happened historically in many European countries. Great Britain is made up of the Irish, Scots, Welsh, and English. Switzerland has its French, Germans, and Italians. Yugoslavia combines Serbs and Croats.

Because the leaders of Africa think of their new states as nations, and because much of the world regards them as nations, it is not improper to apply the term to Africa's new states. In most of these states the sense of nationhood is very new—and very fragile. In some of them the forces of divisiveness have already contributed to serious internal tensions. Ethnic tensions were a factor in the Nigerian civil war; ethnic conflict has resulted in mass murder in Burundi; and there is armed struggle between ethnic groups in Chad and Ethiopia. Yet no nation-states have yet broken apart, and in most African states the struggle to deepen the sense of nationhood and make it permanent is energetically under way.

This struggle—to deepen the sense of nationhood and ensure its permanence—is one of the most important objectives of African governments. Most African leaders believe that prosperity for their nations cannot be achieved until all the peoples of the nation develop this deeper sense of nationhood and patriotism. The leaders believe, further, that their nations cannot play an effective role in African or world affairs until their citizens are genuinely united in spirit. Great expenditures in men and money are therefore being allocated for what is most often termed "nation building."

As used in modern Africa, "nation building" denotes the effort to raise the educational level of the people; to unite them physically by better transportation and communications; to help them to work cooperatively with each other and with their national government; and to lend a sense of common purpose to their lives.

In the effort of nation building, African nations face several common problems. One is the problem of confused national boundaries. During the colonial partitioning, boundaries were often set arbitrarily, sometimes dividing a large ethnic group between two colonial territories, or else merging quite dissimilar ethnic groups in a common territory. The boundaries themselves were often imprecise, occasioning later disputes between colonial powers and even greater disputes between the independent African nations after the colonial period. For example, Ethiopia, Kenya, Somalia, and France have struggled for years with a bor-

BERBER, MOROCCO

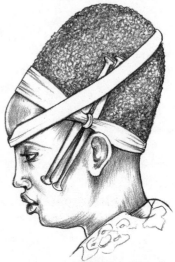

WATUTSI, RWANDA

SWAZI, SWAZILAND

YORUBA, WESTERN NIGERIA

IBO, EASTERN NIGERIA

MOSLEM WOMAN, ALGERIA

der problem which arose when the Somali people were apportioned into Ethiopia, Kenya, Somalia, and Djibouti (French Somaliland). Somalia would like to include in its own national territory all areas in which Somalis now live. But Ethiopia, Kenya, and Djibouti maintain that this would violate their territorial integrity—and that the Somali people living within their boundaries are as Ethiopian, Kenyan, or Djiboutian as any other of the diverse peoples there. Border skirmishes, raids, and military buildups have been common in this struggle, which has resulted in war between Ethiopia and Somalia.

Another problem that many new African nations face is that of a small population scattered over a very large area. This causes severe problems of internal communication. Botswana is a good example. Its 800,000 people, most of whom belong to the Batswana ethnic group, are scattered over 337,000 square miles—an area as large as all of New England plus the state of Texas. Botswana, a poor country, finds it extremely difficult to bridge the great physical distances involved in order to keep its people in communication with each other.

The diverse ethnic composition of many of the new nations of Africa brings serious obstacles to the nation-building effort. Even where the borders of the nation are well defined, the several large ethnic groups within them may have a history of mutual antagonism, and may feel a sense of loyalty to the ethnic group that is as strong as their national loyalty. The members of these ethnic groups may have developed a lively sense of common nationhood, but their differing languages and customs can still create complex problems of internal unity and communication.

Modern education, itself a strong uniting influence,

yet serves to set educated men apart from the unedu-
cated. Thus many of the new nations face a kind of class
conflict, with the educated in one class and the illiterate
in another. It is very difficult to bridge this gap, with the
educated men thinking in Western terms and the uned-
ucated thinking in traditional African terms.

All the new nations of Africa are experiencing an
increasing rural-urban conflict, which again acts as a
handicap to nation building. The rural people, aware
that their own lives have changed little since independence, resent the development they see in the cities.
The people of the cities in turn feel superior and modern, and are more concerned with their own advancement than with that of the rural areas. The widening
distance between educated and illiterate, between
urban and rural, is found also between young people
and older people. African nations are experiencing a
generation gap of some magnitude, causing tension
and lack of communication. The older people live a
traditional way of life; the younger people are attracted
to a modern way of life.

There are two aspects of the nation-building effort
now going on in the new African nations. The first
aspect is the formal programs started by the governments of the new nations. In such programs, the leadership of the nation (including the elected government
officials, the leaders of the chief political parties, and
men of high public standing) consciously initiates projects that strengthen the nation-building effort.
Speeches are made; roads are built; radio and television
shows are produced; schools are expanded; and the
leaders tour the country to stress the need for unity and
a sense of nationhood.

The other aspect of the nation-building effort is an
unplanned one: the vast process of change that all Afri-

can nations are now undergoing. New beliefs are replacing old; new values are being introduced; new institutions of government and law are gradually being accepted; and new patterns of leadership and authority at the national level are gradually replacing those at the village and ethnic level. The occurrence of these changes is, more frequently than not, of aid in nation building.

Public confidence in the newly elected leadership seemed almost unanimous at the start. Yet within a short period of years, in some of the new nations, the picture has changed. Many governments have fallen in military coups. Evidence of unrest is widespread. Progress toward prosperity, especially among the mass of people, is disappointing. Governments have resorted to increasingly stern measures to suppress opposition.

Every government in independent Africa is faced with demands from the people that it cannot meet without a national public consensus. The people must have confidence in the government. They must subordinate some immediate interests and be willing to work for the satisfaction of long-range national interests.

Prior to independence the major force working toward national unity was the nationalist party. The party usually originated in the city, and quickly acquired support from urban groups: labor unions, schoolteachers, students, clerks, marketwomen and tradesmen, ex-servicemen, and other "modernized" people. The party then spread into the rural areas, where, working through the village schoolteachers, the district clerks, the ex-servicemen, and even the schoolchildren, it established an effective relationship with the majority of the people.

The nationalist political movement had an immediate goal: to cast out the colonial rulers and give power to the Africans. The African leaders would then bring Africa into a dignified place in the world community and would provide access to the money, the education, the health services, and the goods that the mass of the people desired.

But this drive for independence obscured, for the moment, the other great problems that lay ahead. Under the surface were the rivalry for authority between the traditional chiefs and the new national leaders; the great disparity, in viewpoint and methods, between the countryside and the modern cities; tensions between various groups within each nation; and powerful neocolonialist forces that served to slow African unity and progress.

At first the new independent governments were able to demonstrate progress to their people. Schools were established, and roads built. Great projects to develop the chief cities were started. Each new African nation joined the United Nations and made forthright statements of its international policy. Ambitious three-year, five-year, and even seven-year national development plans were unveiled. New bank notes and coins were put into circulation. National airlines were started. The leaders moved into the grand official residences of the outgoing colonial dignitaries. Impressive public ceremonies and parades were organized. National stadiums for athletic events and civic observances were built. Africans, elected by Africans, had come into their own

—and they wanted to show that they could spend more and produce more than their alien predecessors.

But this initial effort was costly, in both money and talent. To staff the government offices with Africans, the new leaders had to call in many of the men and women who had run the political party, the schools, and other institutions. To fill their former jobs, inexperienced and often less effective people were recruited from the ranks. In many of the new nations communication between the top leaders and the central political party quickly deteriorated.

In the same process the energy that the most effective political leaders had once devoted to communicating with and inspiring the people was now directed to the problems of government. These leaders became isolated from the people—their source of strength.

At the same time, government budgets quickly expanded to meet the costs of modernization. But this required additional income, which could come only from reserve funds, from higher taxes and duties, or from foreign aid. Because foreign aid was inadequate, reserve funds and domestic revenues had to be used. The mass of people resented higher taxes and duties because they had not yet been able to increase their earnings. Faced with mounting taxes and costs, yet seeing little economic progress, the people's confidence in their government and their national spirit quickly declined.

This process can be illustrated by what has happened in Ghana and Tanzania. These two countries, faced with similar problems of nation building, have tried different solutions.

In Ghana, the great nationalist leader Kwame Nkrumah led the nation to freedom with impressive national support and unity. And Ghana entered independence

SENUFO,
UPPER VOLTA

CAMEROON

GELEDE SOCIETY,
NIGERIA

BOBO, UPPER VOLTA

SENUFO,
IVORY COAST

BAPENDE, ZAIRE

with enormous reserve funds and one of the most prosperous economic systems in Africa.

Rapid expansion took place in schools, roads, health
services, port facilities, and industry. But from the out-
set Nkrumah followed a policy of strong central power,
and suppressed opposition and dissent. He also supported the pan-Africanist ideology and used Ghanaian
funds, manpower, and talents to influence political developments in other parts of the continent.

Aggravated by outside influences, internal dissension
increased. There was a large urban unemployment
problem, a continuing struggle by sectional groups to
gain a share of power, and a deteriorating financial
situation. Nkrumah's response was to increase his own
power. The opposition political party was outlawed.
One by one, its leaders were jailed without trial. The
newspapers were censored. The national radio became
a propaganda organ. Nkrumah encouraged a kind of
deification of himself, and had himself declared president for life. As time went on, Nkrumah jailed leaders
in his own party for real or suspected disloyalty. He
became a tightly guarded recluse, surrounded by a
handpicked army and living in a fortresslike palace.

Ghana's enormous financial reserves were at last
gone, and debts piled up. There was hope that some of
Nkrumah's programs would ultimately pay off and
strengthen Ghana's economy. But much money had
been spent on projects that were economically useless:
statues, public squares and parade grounds, unneces-
sary government buildings, resort homes for political
leaders, superhighways that were seldom used. World
prices for Ghana's products declined, and the great
powers of the West showed their deep hostility toward
Nkrumah and his policies.

Finally the army, deeply concerned with the country's

financial plight and its totalitarian government, seized power while Nkrumah was visiting China. His party was abolished; its cabinet ministers were removed from office; and political prisoners were released.

It is difficult to tell yet whether Nkrumah's leadership weakened or strengthened Ghana's national spirit. Succeeding governments have begun to praise his program. He failed—but his very failure may have increased the national determination to succeed.

JULIUS NYERERE
OF TANZANIA

A very different effort was made on the other side of the continent in Tanganyika (called today Tanzania, since its union with Zanzibar). Like Nkrumah, Tanzania's Julius Nyerere and his Tanganyika African National Union led the country to independence with widespread support from the people. But in Tanzania, in contrast with Ghana, there were no serious internal tensions except those between the African population and the immigrant Asian community.

Nyerere's government also launched a diversified program for national development. Schools have been expanded, new roads built, health services improved—and the national debt has risen somewhat. But all these efforts have been more modest and cautious than in Ghana.

Nyerere consistently has discouraged any attempt to glorify his person or his position. Concerned about the danger of losing touch with the people, he has frequently traveled throughout the country to speak with people of all types. At one point, not long after independence, he resigned as head of the government in order to devote a year to rebuilding the political party and strengthening his ties with the people. At the end of the year, he was reelected president by an almost unanimous vote.

Tanzania, with no real opposition political movement, has also become a one-party state. But it has encouraged a degree of discussion and dissenting opinion within the one party. The legal prerogative to jail opposition leaders exists, but it has rarely been used.

Tanzania's leaders stress simplicity and austerity in their personal conduct. They dress plainly, occupy relatively modest homes, and are not allowed by the party to accumulate wealth. The party urges a policy of self-reliance and egalitarianism for the people; and the leaders are required to set an example.

In almost every new African nation the government is headed by a man who came to power as (in a sense) the "father of his country." African political leaders feel strongly that it is essential, if a new government is to be effective, to have one man at its head in whom all the people can have confidence, regardless of their ethnic group, age, sex, wealth, education, religion, or occupation. The national leader is often a member of a minority group, so that he does not arouse fears that he might favor one section over the others.

To a certain extent, the idea of a strong national leader is traditional in Africa. Many of Africa's peoples are accustomed to being ruled by a king or chief—some of whom have even been deified. But in a time of great change and uncertainty, the desire for a strong leader is almost universal. This produces a tremendous temptation for the leader to take personal advantage of his power. Nkrumah is not the only African leader who has tried to enrich himself and to make his position permanent. But there are other leaders, like Nyerere, who have honored the trust bestowed on them: Kaunda of Zambia, Khama of Botswana, Touré of Guinea.

Every new African nation has felt that it needs a government that is strong, centralized, and virtually unchallenged. Although Africa wants the respect of demo-

cratic countries elsewhere, the African people in the
main are not accustomed to a democratic system of
government based on the voting process and on political parties. Africa has generally not been antidemo-
cratic or totalitarian; but it has been traditionalistic.
Time-honored beliefs and ways of behavior bound all
members of society, including the elders, chiefs, and
kings. The leaders had authority to interpret and en-
force conformity to custom; but they were not free to
act arbitrarily and without restraint. Today the individual raised in traditional African society finds the idea of
democracy attractive, but tends to prefer it to be exercised in African terms, rather than in competing political parties or Western parliamentary government structures.

Perhaps the most dramatic and vigorous effort tran-
spiring in modern Africa is the expansion of formal
education. Illiterate farmers in the most remote areas,
often resisting change for themselves, demand schools
for their children. Formal, Western-type education is a
powerful instrument of change. The African child, after
a few years of schooling, learns to read and write a
European language, and eventually to think in that language. He learns mathematics, then moves on to a
grounding in the scientific method of explaining the
world around him. He studies world geography and
world history, and reads the works of famous European
thinkers. After a few years his "African" way of thinking
is fundamentally changed. No longer can he accept the
sayings of his elders without question. No longer can he
live, day to day, the same life that his parents and grand-
parents have lived.

The effect of education on the child is well known to
his parents and relatives; yet they encourage him to

To Tia & Tio
James Brendon Lusan
9 months

become educated. They know that he will become in part a stranger, questioning and challenging the beliefs by which they live. Yet they see education as the key to the better life—and they mean for their children to have that life, regardless of the consequences.

The average African views education as the way to wealth, high position, and dignity in the modern world. The leaders of the new nations view it as essential because the educated person is, in a way, freed from narrow sectional beliefs and loyalties, and becomes a contributing member of the modern nation.

Many countries devote as much as 20 percent of their entire national budget to education; Nigeria's Western Region at one point was spending over 40 percent. In most of the new nations additional primary schools were built even before there were qualified teachers for them. Several countries (for example, Ghana, Nigeria, Kenya, and Ivory Coast) have provided places for 80 to 90 percent of all school-age children. But this expansion has resulted in a lower quality of primary schooling, because the schools had to be staffed by poorly qualified teachers.

Secondary schools have also multiplied—but not so rapidly as the primary schools. Most African countries have remained tied to the British or French secondary-school philosophy. To be graduated from secondary school, the student takes a national final examination similar to the British Cambridge School Certificate or the French Baccalauréat. Therefore the secondary schools must have qualified teachers, so that the students can pass these stiff examinations.

In several African countries there are only ten secondary-school openings for every hundred primary-school graduates; that is, ninety of every hundred students have no opportunity for further education. But after finishing six to eight years of primary school, the youth are too modernized to be content with the impoverished rural life of their parents. They flock to the towns and cities, seeking jobs or educational opportunities, and add to the already serious unemployment problem. There are not enough jobs in any of Africa's cities for the large numbers who come to seek them.

Most African nations have sacrificed much to establish a national university. And thousands of Africa's young men and women have gone to universities all over the world to continue their education.

Educational expansion has been so rapid that African nations have paid little attention to the quality and content of the education provided to their young people. All of Africa's new nations have continued, without much modification, the educational system laid down by European missionaries and governments during the colonial period. It is a basically academic education, not sufficiently related to African social and economic conditions. Students who finish their formal education in Africa shun the rural, traditional environment and seek the new urban environment. They have little understanding of their own society. Their education has not equipped them to fill the present needs of their society. The educational system does not yet offer enough technical and vocational training that can be put to immediate use. The African student sometimes cannot find useful employment.

The best educational opportunities have developed in or near the cities. The best opportunities for earning a living are now also in or near the cities. Large sums have been spent in the cities by government for hospitals, recreation facilities, buildings, streets, and a variety of urban services. Political activity concentrates in

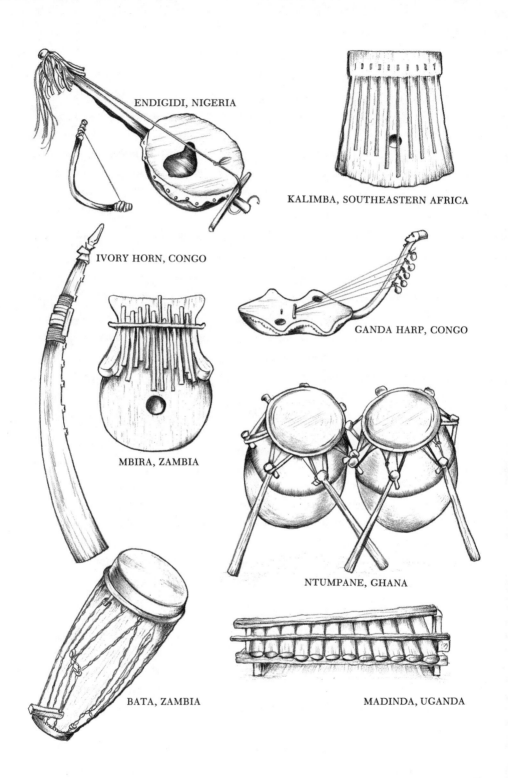

ENDIGIDI, NIGERIA

KALIMBA, SOUTHEASTERN AFRICA

IVORY HORN, CONGO

GANDA HARP, CONGO

MBIRA, ZAMBIA

NTUMPANE, GHANA

BATA, ZAMBIA

MADINDA, UGANDA

the city. And it is in the city that the nongovernmental social organizations flourish: youth groups, women's groups, labor unions, and social-service associations.

The rural areas suffer in this process. The new African nations are urban nations; and the strong national consciousness evident in the cities decreases as distance from the city increases. To the extent that the nation-building process influences the rural areas, it is greatest along the railroad lines and major highways and in the areas lying between two cities. Other rural areas are largely left out.

Many African governments have attempted major youth-organization projects to help solve the urban unemployment problem; to bring national consciousness and progress to the rural areas; and to alleviate the frustrations of educated youth. Inspired to a certain extent by similar, successful foreign programs, such as Israel's youth movements, America's Peace Corps, and various Communist youth corps, almost all the new nations have experimented in this area. The Ghana Builder's Brigade, the Tanzania National Youth Service, the Zambia Youth Service Corps, and many other efforts have had parallel concerns and hopes. Most of these organizations have trained youth in manual skills and awareness of national goals, and then have sent them to land settlement projects or village improvement projects. Although none of these experiments has yet been wholly successful, youth organizations are still thought to have great potential for doing good.

Africa's horizons, limited for countless centuries by the Sahara Desert and the seas, have been incredibly widened in the past century by new ideas, new goods, a new technology, and a new knowledge of the world at large. The changes sweeping Africa will ultimately produce a different continent. Age-old beliefs are giving way to new ones or are going through a process of adaptation to the changing times. Modern Africans are in transition, moving between the old way and the new way; and to a very large extent, they are trying to embrace both simultaneously.

For many years to come, Africa is likely to be a restless, turbulent continent. Most of the nations being built will grow into permanent, unified societies. But the path cannot be smooth. Africa has embarked on a course of profound change—and the end is not yet in sight.

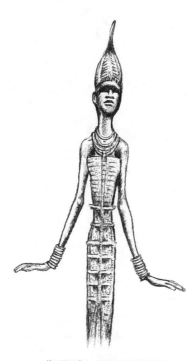

"AFRICA AWAKENING"
—CONTEMPORARY SCULPTURE BY BEN ENWONWU

◄9►

Africa's Role in World Affairs

The African relationship with the former colonial powers is a complex one, combining attitudes of hostility, respect, resentment, gratitude, sensitivity, and confidence. Africa surged to independence with much anti-European feeling; but most of the new nations have continued at least a minimally cordial relationship with the former colonial powers.

Various Western nations that have had no recent part in exploiting African colonial territories—such as the United States, West Germany, and Canada—have developed important relationships with Africa's new nations. Relations between the United States and the new African nations, for example, were begun with substantial goodwill on both sides. Africans had a favorable opinion of the United States because of its historic commitment to democracy and freedom. They observed, in the years immediately prior to their independence, that the United States did not support the principle of colonial rule with any enthusiasm. The tremendous wealth of the United States and the generosity with which it had helped Europe to recover from the devastation of World War II encouraged the African states to hope that they might receive moral and financial support.

But in the years since independence, relations between America and the African nations have become increasingly complex. Those countries that have benefited from American aid, trade, and investment—such as Liberia, Morocco, Tunisia, and Zaire—tend to value the relationship and to express reasonably friendly feelings toward the United States. But almost all of the countries have developed reservations, because they feel that the United States is playing a global power game and is part of the neocolonial system that still inhibits African freedom and growth.

Throughout Africa there is resentment at continued domination of the black majority in Southern Africa by white minorities. There is a feeling that the West tacitly condones and supports this situation; and the United States, as the leader of the Western world, receives considerable African blame. Africans are also aware that the United States does not regard Africa as important in terms of American strategic interests.

The achievement of independence by African nations helped make white Americans more aware of the plight of black Americans, and encouraged black Americans to intensify their own struggles for equal rights. Just as American policy toward Africa must take at least somewhat into account the black American's attitudes, so the

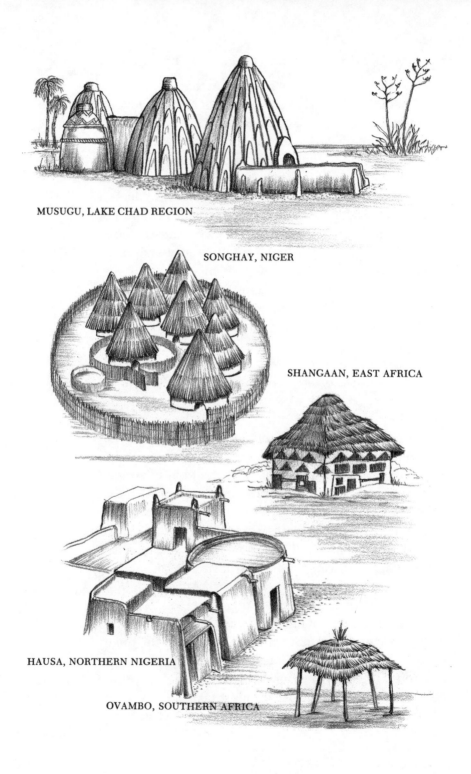

MUSUGU, LAKE CHAD REGION

SONGHAY, NIGER

SHANGAAN, EAST AFRICA

HAUSA, NORTHERN NIGERIA

OVAMBO, SOUTHERN AFRICA

LOANDA, ANGOLA

MANGBETU, ZAIRE

BAGANDA, UGANDA

ZULU, SOUTHERN AFRICA

TONGA, ZAMBIA

policies of Africa's nations toward the United States are influenced by their reaction to the struggles of American blacks. The racial incidents in Birmingham, Alabama, and in Little Rock, Arkansas, received much publicity in Africa and aroused great emotion.

Of the other Western powers, several have developed programs of trade, aid, and amity with the new African nations; these include Australia, Canada, Denmark, Germany, New Zealand, Norway, and Sweden. The African attitude toward these nations (especially the smaller ones, which offer no threat of "neocolonialism") tends to be cordial. Africans have favored relationships with the Scandinavian countries, for example. They impress Africans as being progressive and wealthy, yet free of colonialist tendencies or attitudes of superiority toward Africa.

The small nation of Israel formerly played a lively role in much of Africa. Israel saw in Africa a potential source of diplomatic support in its tense conflict with the Arab world, as well as a market for Israeli manufactured goods. And drawing on her own recent experience in nation building, Israel argued that it understood and sympathized with the struggles of Africa's new nations to find prosperity, to build national pride, and to develop an identity in the world community.

Throughout the 1960's Israel worked hard, with considerable success, to win African support. It sent technicians and military advisors to Africa and developed trade relations with many African states. Relations have deteriorated seriously since the 1967 and Yom Kippur wars between Israel and its Arab neighbors, however, and today most Africans view Israel as an aggressive member of the Western neocolonialist bloc.

The anti-Western stance of Africa's nationalist movements has implied a cordiality toward the East: the socialist countries of the Soviet bloc. Most of Africa's nationalist leaders had read Marx, Lenin, Engels, Stalin, Mao Tse-tung, and other Communist writers during their studies. A few leaders from the French territories had close ties with the French Communist party. Virtually all the nationalists were outspoken in their condemnation of capitalism and their praise of socialism as an economic philosophy.

In the years just before independence, the colonial governments went to great lengths to prevent the possibility of Communist influence in the colonies. No literature from Communist nations was permitted to enter the territory; travel to Communist countries was prohibited; visas were not granted to Soviet and other Communist travelers who wished to visit colonial Africa. To a very large extent Africa was sealed off from the Soviet bloc, except when young Africans studying in Europe and the United States read Communist literature or met Communists. It was frequently assumed that Africans, in their desperate anticolonial drive, would align themselves with the Communist countries against the colonialist West.

There was evidence at the same time that the Soviet Union and its allies in Eastern Europe had considerable interest in Africa, particularly during the Cold War era. Some of the minerals of Africa were in short supply in the Soviet bloc countries. The few Africans who traveled to these countries were lionized. Communist leaders, newspapers, and radios constantly denounced colonialism and praised the efforts of Africans to throw it off.

However, since Africa's new nations have become independent, surprisingly little Eastern influence has developed. The majority of new African nations have welcomed diplomatic relations, trade, technical assistance and loan programs, and cultural exchanges with the East; but this has resulted in few real alignments or alliances.

Most of Africa's new nations came into independence with a foreign policy based on nonalignment, or neutralism. In their urgent search for a specifically African identity, the new nations have felt—with few exceptions —that they must remain free of any foreign domination or entanglement. The African attitude is very similar to the American attitude of the late eighteenth century, after the United States became independent of colonial rule.

This attitude of nonalignment has been directed at the Eastern world almost as much as at the Western world. Many diplomats, from both East and West, have had rude surprises when they made their first attempts to develop influence in Africa. When Guinea became independent, for example, the Soviet Union was one of the first to come to its aid. The Soviets sent in a quantity of money, technicians, advisors, and machinery, amid great cordiality and goodwill. But in 1961, as soon as the Soviet ambassador began to meddle in Guinea's internal affairs, he was promptly expelled, and a period of cool relations followed.

The same African pragmatism that has maintained good relations with the former colonial powers has regulated affairs between Africa and the East. Where a socialist nation is helpful and not too demanding, the relationship is good. Where it is too demanding or not helpful, the relationship is likely to be strained or broken.

The Soviet Union and other Eastern European countries have given considerable assistance to some African nations. Soviet aid has occasionally produced flashy, showpiece projects that are expected to bring quick political returns. But more often, they are projects that Africans seriously want and need.

As things stand, after a few years of direct contact between African nations and the socialist world, there is a fairly balanced, low-key relationship. No African countries have rejected orderly relations characterized by mutual respect; but neither have any "gone Communist" or thrown in their lot with the East. This is not to say that all African nations have had the same experience with Soviet bloc countries, or that attitudes are the same in all the independent nations. Some African nations have shown only a minimal, polite interest in the East—and the relationship in these cases is minor and unimportant. Good examples are Ivory Coast and Madagascar. Some African nations, on the other hand, have deliberately sought stronger ties with the Soviet Union or Soviet bloc countries for economic or political reasons. Ghana under Nkrumah, Egypt, Algeria, and Congo (Brazzaville) are examples.

African relations with China have been very complex. China has not played a major role in most African countries, but it has increasingly become a force in eastern and Southern Africa. It made a major loan to Tanzania and Zambia to build a railroad linking the two, thus providing Zambia with a new, vitally important outlet to the sea. China has also provided assistance to African liberation movements in Southern Africa. During the late 1960's and early 1970's, these efforts helped make China very popular in Africa.

China's new relationship with the United States has, since 1973, resulted in a loss of Chinese influence in Africa. This grew especially obvious in 1975 when China, the United States, and South Africa jointly intervened in Angola's civil war, supporting nationalist forces who proved to have little popular support. The more popular movement, the MPLA, was supported by the Soviet Union and Cuba; the latter sent troops to help win the war. Most Africans favored the MPLA in this struggle, and criticized the United States and China for their intervention and for their association with South Africa.

It is unlikely that China will play a major role in Africa for the foreseeable future. It does not have the financial and manpower resources to do so, and Africa is not regarded as being of high strategic importance to China. It can, however, expand its influence in Africa if it does not link itself too closely with the United States in joint ventures such as the fiasco in Angola.

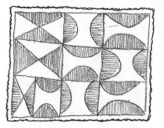

There has been a striking contrast distinguishing Africa in the middle of the twentieth century. On the one hand, there has been a marked similarity of thought and attitude—of ideology—among the African nationalists who led their nations to independence. And on the other hand, each nation has been separated from its neighbors by great obstacles of language, communications, and form of government.

One of the most basic tenets of African nationalism has been pan-Africanism, or African unity; and each new nation has professed to want greater unity with other African nations. The three East Africa nations of Kenya, Tanzania, and Uganda long maintained close regional ties that began in colonial days under the East

African High Commission. For several years they had a common currency, a joint airline and postal system, and other similar linkages. Independence and the effort to develop within each country have seriously weakened this unity, however, and most of the joint enterprises have been abandoned.

The former French territories have also developed a number of regional groupings for cooperation in education, research, communications, and tariff setting. Although these efforts to achieve greater unity have been limited, they remain in existence, and most of the French-speaking states still belong to an Organisation Commune Africaine, Malgache et Mauricienne, which binds them together loosely.

The most durable effort at African unity has been the Organization for African Unity—founded in 1963—to which all the independent nations in Africa (except the Republic of South Africa) belong. The OAU maintains a permanent secretariat in Addis Ababa, Ethiopia, and

TINABU SQUARE, LAGOS, NIGERIA

coordinates a number of intra-African interests. The policies of the OAU are set at periodic meetings of the heads of its member states. The OAU has served a useful role in easing border disputes between member states and in coordinating African efforts to resist apartheid and colonialism in Southern Africa.

Since independence, most African nations have had to concern themselves with internal problems and so have not found it possible to merge into larger national states or federations. A few unions have been attempted. Some of these have quickly fallen apart, such as the Mali Federation between Senegal and the former French Soudan (now called Mali), and a Ghana-Guinea union. But others have been more successful: the merger of Tanganyika and Zanzibar into the United Republic of Tanzania has survived, as has the merger of British and Italian Somaliland into Somalia; the British Cameroons and the French Cameroun into Cameroon; and the union of British Togoland with Ghana. It is likely that further efforts at formal African unity will be made, although they will probably be in the nature of common markets, customs unions, or communications unions, rather than new political federations.

African nations have joined the United Nations and have participated in its affairs with great enthusiasm. Together the African nations form the largest regional grouping in the UN. African states see their UN membership as a formal symbol of acceptance, as equals, into the world community, and use their UN seats as a way to speak out, and be heard, on issues that they consider important. These include the ending of colonialism, the freeing of black majorities from white minority rule, and the rapid advancement of underdeveloped areas.

It must not be assumed that African nations agree on

everything, either at home or in the UN. Their votes on most issues in the UN fall on both sides, despite an active African caucus in which they discuss their stands before a vote is called.

In addition to valuing the UN as a forum and a symbol of membership in the world community, African nations have very high regard for its technical assistance programs and its coordinating role in public health improvement, tariff agreements, agricultural and scientific research, and other areas. Most African nations prefer to receive assistance through the UN rather than directly from other countries, because UN aid carries no threat of foreign domination.

In a few short years Africa's new nations have learned rapidly the responsibilities of being members of the world community, and most have found it possible to build good relations with both the East and the West.

◀ 10 ▶

Africa Faces the Future

Africans have not created a "brave new world" since independence; but neither have they failed. In many countries the people have done all that could realistically have been expected—and more.

Many Africans, when they first won independence, had as unrealistic an idea of their future problems as Americans and Europeans once had. Africa's leaders constantly proclaimed to their peoples that freedom would mean speedy progress. Colonial administrators, in the main, had been there only to administer—not to lead in the development of underdeveloped lands. At their best, the colonial leaders were thoughtful, wise, skilled, and often of very good will. But they took few risks, and felt little of the urgency that Africans them-selves felt about their situation.

National independence brought to every new African nation a flood of fresh energy—energy that under colo-nial rule was suppressed or was directed toward eject-ing the colonial powers. Now budgets were increased; massive foreign aid was sought; and a great sense of urgency was manifest.

African leaders have made many mistakes. Precious funds have been wasted on uneconomic businesses and development schemes. Much has been spent on display projects that should have gone for long-term develop-ment. Graft, corruption, and dishonesty have plagued a number of countries. A few countries have ap-proached the brink of bankruptcy, staggering under the burden of heavy loans for developments that will take many years to pay off.

Yet despite mistakes, failures, and waste, great prog-ress has been made—and is continuing. Thousands of miles of new or improved roads have been built. Educa-tional facilities have multiplied. Profitable industries have been established. Dams, hydroelectric stations, new bridges, and irrigation schemes have appeared in almost every African nation. And most important of all, thousands of Africans are learning from their mistakes and building up a store of sorely needed experience.

It is difficult to overemphasize the handicaps that have faced African nations in their critical shortage of trained, experienced people. At the time of indepen-dence, only a handful of Africans had acquired adminis-trative experience in government. These untried lead-ers usually felt that they could not continue to rely on the help of the colonial civil servants and technical ex-perts. They eagerly seized opportunities to train young Africans, and recruited noncolonial helpers from the

United Nations, the United States, the Soviet Union, and dozens of other technologically advanced countries.

The flow of aid, loans, and investment into Africa has been disappointingly small. Foreign powers often give as much advice as financial assistance. Rarely a day passes that the average African minister of education does not have several visitors from abroad—each with a new set of ideas about how he should reform his education system. Americans criticize the system the British left behind and extol the American approach; the Scandinavians commend their own system; the Russians emphasize theirs.

Foreign aid often has strings attached—not, usually, crude political requirements, but more subtle ones, such as expecting the new nation to match the aid funds, to prepare elaborate project proposals, or to use costly technicians and equipment from the donor country. Thus, simply accepting aid costs African nations money, crucial skilled manpower, and badly needed time.

One African leader, Julius Nyerere of Tanzania, has proclaimed a national policy of self-reliance. It calls on Tanzanians to build their nation with their own labor, money, and skills. President Nyerere has pointed out to his people that foreign aid is too small in amount and too difficult to obtain for the nation to rely on it.

Tanzania has begun to face a hard fact that all African nations must face. African expectations of dramatic help from other countries are slowly fading, and the leaders are trying to prepare their people for the long, difficult march toward a better future—a march that must be made by the Africans themselves.

This is the state of current African thinking. The leaders and the people are beginning to recognize the true nature and size of their problems. With this recognition comes the knowledge that the job of building Africa—piece by piece, day by day—is Africa's. Foreign help is needed and will yet play a part, but it is not the first necessity. As Africa now faces the future, several basic lessons are being learned.

First, African nations are heavily rural and agricultural in nature; hence more effort is needed to guide rural development. Most of the new nations have first turned their attention to the cities, to industry, to academic education, to the central government, and to foreign relations. But these are not the most important things. There is a growing sense that most African nations will be primarily rural—and dependent on better agriculture—for many years to come.

Second, the education upon which all African nations so heavily depend is gradually being recognized as ill suited to the present needs and conditions of African society. Based on European ideas of education of the late nineteenth and early twentieth centuries, African systems of education are largely academic and semiclassical in nature. They have as their main goal the preparation of the child for university study—not for life in a rural, rapidly developing nation. Driven by necessity, a number of African nations are beginning educational reforms. They are seeking ways of adapting their recently expanded school systems to the immediate needs of African society, but progress has been very slow in creating genuinely African-oriented education.

Third, African governments are beginning to see the need for a renewed spirit of dedication and understanding on the part of their government leaders. They are growing conscious (at least in some nations) of the lack of communication between the leaders and the majority of their people. They are realizing that the leaders must set an example that the people can follow. Several governments have been overthrown in revulsion against the wealth and grand living style that their leaders have displayed at the expense of their people. Other leaders are learning that the peoples of Africa demand good leadership if they are to be led at all.

Fourth, some African leaders have learned from their own mistakes and the mistakes of others. There are admittedly many who are corrupt or ineffective, who retain power by force. But there is a growing number of administrative and political leaders of great ability and sound experience.

Africa faces the future with high hopes. Its hopes are more attuned to reality now than they were at the start of independence. Few people in Africa expect miracles or overnight transformation.

The rest of the world needs to acquire the more realistic view of Africa that Africa itself has developed. Governments have changed suddenly in Africa; and they will do so in the future. Progress will be made, but it will appear to be slow at times. Nations will gradually grow stronger, but there will be tensions and unrest. Africa for the next few years may not be peaceful, sedate, and orderly—but it will not fall apart.

Paradoxically, the tensions, the instabilities, the unrest are really signs of progress in Africa. Africa is alive and in the process of dynamic change. Its people are on the march. They are throwing off centuries of isolation.

They are hungry for progress and for a place in an exciting world.

No one can predict for a hundred years ahead. In the flux of revolutionary change that is modern Africa, one can hardly predict for even a decade ahead. But the signs for Africa are favorable. The African people are alert and eager, and possessed of great native ability. African resources are substantial. African leaders are able and are learning rapidly. Together, these advantages can carry Africa to a bright future.

Selected Reading List

GENERAL BOOKS ON AFRICA

American Society of African Culture. *Africa Seen by American Negroes.* New York, 1960.

Bernheim, Marc and Evelyne. *From Bush to City: A Look at the New Africa.* New York, Harcourt, Brace & World, 1966.

Bohannon, Paul and Philip Curtin. *Africa and the Africans.* New York, Natural History Press, 1971.

Lengyel, Emil. *Africa: Past, Present and Future.* New York, Oxford, 1966.

Singleton, F. Seth, and Shingler, John. *Africa in Perspective.* New York, Hayden Book Co., 1967.

Thompson, Elizabeth B. *Contemporary Africa: Continent in Transition.* Boston, Houghton Mifflin, 1966.

LAND AND PEOPLES

Brom, John L. *African Odyssey.* New York, Living Books, 1966.

Carr, Archie F., and the editors of *Life* Magazine. *The Land and Wildlife of Africa.* New York, Time, Inc., 1964.

Clark, Leon E. (ed.). *Through African Eyes.* New York, Praeger, 1969.

Drachler, Jacob (ed.). *African Heritage: Intimate Views of the Black Africans from Life, Love, and Literature.* New York, Collier, 1964.

Feldman, Susan. *African Myths and Tales.* New York, Dell Publishing Co., 1963.

Hodgson, Robert D., and Elvyn A. Stoneman. *The Changing Map of Africa.* Princeton, N.J., Van Nostrand, 1964.

Nolen, Barbara (ed.). *Africa Is People.* New York, Dutton, 1967.

Ojigbo, A. Okion. *Young and Black in Africa.* New York, Random House, 1971.

Vlahos, Olivia. *African Beginnings.* New York, Viking Press, 1967.

White, Jo Ann. *African Views of the West.* New York, Messner, 1972.

HISTORY

Bovill, E. W., *The Golden Trade of the Moors.* London, Oxford University Press, 1968.

Brown, L. *Africa: A Natural History.* London, Hamilton, 1965.

Davidson, Basil. *The African Past: Chronicles from Antiquity to Modern Times.* Boston, Little, Brown, 1964.

———. *Black Mother: The Years of the African Slave Trade.* Boston, Little, Brown, 1961.

———. *The Lost Cities of Africa.* Boston, Little, Brown, 1963.

———, and the editors of Time-Life Books. *African Kingdoms.* New York, Time, Inc., 1966.

Dobler, Lavinia, and William A. Brown. *Great Rulers of the African Past.* Garden City, N.Y., Doubleday, 1966.

Edwards, Paul (ed.). *Equiano's Travels.* New York, Praeger, 1966.

Horizon Books (eds.). *The Horizon History of Africa.* New York, American Heritage, 1972.

Killingray, David. *A Plague of Europeans.* Harmondsworth, Penguin, 1973.

Knight, Frank. *Stories of Famous Explorers by Land.* Philadelphia, Westminster, 1966.

Murphy, E. Jefferson. *The Bantu Civilization of Southern Africa.* New York, Crowell, 1974.

————. *History of African Civilization.* New York, Crowell, 1972.

Oliver, Roland, and Caroline Oliver (eds.). *Africa in the Days of Exploration.* Englewood Cliffs, N.J., Prentice-Hall, 1965.

Oliver, Roland, and John D. Fage. *A Short History of Africa.* Baltimore, Penguin, 1962.

Perham, Marjorie, and Jack Simmons (eds.). *African Discovery: An Anthology of Exploration.* London, Faber & Faber, 1957.

Shinnie, Margaret. *Ancient African Kingdoms.* New York, St. Martin's, 1965.

Sterling, Thomas, and the editors of *Horizon* Magazine. *Exploration of Africa.* New York, American Heritage, 1963.

POLITICS, GOVERNMENT, AND LEADERS

Adams, Russell L. *Great Negroes, Past and Present.* Chicago, Afro-American Publishing Co., 1963.

Crane, Louise. *Ms. Africa: Profiles of Modern African Women.* Philadelphia, Lippincott, 1973.

Evans, Lancelot O. (ed.). *Emerging African Nations and Their Leaders* (2 vols.). Yonkers, N.Y., Educational Heritage (Negro Heritage Library), 1964.

Kaula, Edna M. *Leaders of the New Africa.* Cleveland, World, 1966.

Legum, Colin. *Pan-Africanism: A Short Political Guide* (rev. ed.). New York, Praeger, 1965.

Lynch, Hollis R. *Edward Wilmot Blyden: Pan-Negro Patriot.* London, Oxford University Press, 1967.

McKown, Robin. *Lumumba.* Garden City, N.Y., Doubleday, 1969.

————. *Nkrumah.* Garden City, N.Y., Doubleday, 1973.

Melady, Thomas P. *The Revolution of Color.* New York, Hawthorn, 1966.

Ngugi, James. *Weep Not, Child.* New York, Fawcett World Library, 1968.

Odinga, Oginga. *Not Yet Uhuru.* New York, Hill & Wang, 1967.

Polatnick, Florence T., and Alberta L. Saletan. *Zambia's President, Kenneth Kaunda.* New York, Messner, 1972.

Smith, William Edgett. *We Must Run While They Walk: A Portrait of Africa's Julius Nyerere.* New York, Random House, 1971.

AFRICAN ARTS

Dick-Read, Robert. *Sanamu: Adventures in Search of African Art.* New York, Dutton, 1964.

Glubok, Shirley. *The Art of Africa.* New York, Harper & Row, 1965.

Marshall, Anthony D. *Africa's Living Arts.* New York, Watts, 1970.

Naylor, Penelope. *Black Images: The Art of West Africa.* Garden City, N.Y., Doubleday, 1973.

Nolen, Barbara. *Africa Is Thunder and Wonder.* New York, Scribner's, 1972.

Price, Christine. *Made in West Africa.* New York, Dutton, 1975.

Serwadda, W. Moses (translated and edited by Hewitt Pantaleoni). *Songs and Stories from Uganda.* New York, Crowell, 1974.

Warren, Fred, and Lee Warren. *The Music of Africa.* Englewood Cliffs, N.J., Prentice-Hall, 1970.

Willet, Frank. *African Art.* New York, Praeger, 1971.

NORTH AND NORTHEAST AFRICA

Baulin, Jacques. *The Arab Role in Africa.* Baltimore, Penguin, 1962.

Brace, Richard M. *Morocco, Algeria, Tunisia.* Englewood Cliffs, N.J., Prentice-Hall, 1964.

Collins, D. A. *A Tear for Somalia: A Story of Life in Somaliland.* London, Jarrolds, 1960.

El-Mahdi, Mandour. *A Short History of the Sudan.* London, Oxford, 1965.

Henderson, K. D. D. *The Sudan Republic.* London, E. Benn, 1965.

Jones, A. H. M., and Elizabeth Monroe. *A Short History of Ethiopia.* London, Oxford, 1968.

Kaula, Edna. *The Land and People of Ethiopia.* Philadelphia, Lippincott, 1965.

Perl, Lila. *Ethiopia, Land of the Lion.* New York, Morrow, 1972.

EAST AFRICA AND MADAGASCAR

Bell, C. R. V. *The Road to Independence: A Certificate History of East Africa.* London, Longman, 1966.

Davidson, Basil, and J. Mhina. *East and Central Africa to the Nineteenth Century.* Garden City, N.Y., Doubleday, 1969.

Kent, Raymond. *From Madagascar to the Malagasy Republic.* New York, Praeger, 1962.

Kenyatta, Jomo. *Facing Mount Kenya.* New York, Random House, 1962.

Marsh, Zoe, and G. W. Kingsnorth. *An Introduction to the History of East Africa.* Cambridge, The University Press, 1966.

p'Bitek, Okot. *Song of Lawinia.* Evanston, Ill., Northwestern University Press, 1966.

Stratton, Arthur. *The Great Red Island.* New York, Scribner's, 1964.

WEST AFRICA

Achebe, Chinua. *No Longer at Ease.* Greenwich, Conn., Fawcett, 1975.

———. *Things Fall Apart.* Greenwich, Conn., Fawcett, 1976.

Bertol, Roland. *Sundiata: The Epic of the Lion King.* New York, Crowell, 1970.

Bohannon, Laura. *Return to Laughter.* Garden City, N.Y., Doubleday, 1964.

Chu, Daniel, and Elliott Skinner. *A Glorious Age in Africa*. Garden City, N.Y., Doubleday, 1965.

Davidson, Basil (with F. K. Buah and J. F. Ade Ajayi). *A History of West Africa to the Nineteenth Century*. Garden City, N.Y., Doubleday, 1968.

Fage, John D. *A History of West Africa*. New York, Cambridge, 1971.

Gay, John. *Red Dust on the Green Leaves*. Thompson, Conn., Interculture Associates, 1973.

Hallett, Robin. *People and Progress in West Africa: an Introduction to the Problems of Development*. New York, Praeger, 1966.

Jenness, Aylette. *Along the Niger River*. New York, Crowell, 1974.

CENTRAL AND SOUTHERN AFRICA

Africa Research Group. *Race to Power*. Boston, Africa Research Group, 1970.

Abrahams, Peter. *Tell Freedom: Memories of Africa*. New York, Knopf, 1954.

Cole, Ernest. *House of Bondage*. New York, Random House, 1967.

Hopkinson, Tom, and the editors of *Life* Magazine. *South Africa*. New York, Time, Inc., 1964.

Kaunda, Kenneth. *Zambia Shall Be Free*. London, Heinemann, 1962.

Legum, Colin, and Margaret Legum. *The Bitter Choice: Eight South Africans' Resistance to Tyranny*. Cleveland, World, 1968.

Marquard, Leo. *The Peoples and Policies of South Africa*. London, Oxford, 1969.

McKown, Robin. *Crisis in South Africa*. New York, Putnam's, 1972.

Minter, William. *Portuguese Africa and the West*. Baltimore, Penguin, 1972.

Mitchison, Naomi. *Friends and Enemies*. New York, John Day, 1968.

Modisane, Bloke. *Blame Me on History*. New York, Dutton, 1963.

Mondlane, Eduardo. *The Struggle for Mozambique*. Baltimore, Penguin, 1969.

Paton, Alan. *The Land and People of South Africa* (rev. ed.). Philadelphia, Lippincott, 1964.

Stein, Harry. *Southern Africa*. New York, Watts, 1975.

Tindall, P. E. H. *A History of Central Africa*. New York, Praeger, 1968.

Wills, A. J. *The History of Central Africa*. London, Oxford, 1967.

Index

E. Jefferson Murphy lives in Amherst, Massachusetts, where he is the coordinator of the Five Colleges, a union of Amherst, Hampshire, Mount Holyoke, and Smith colleges and the University of Massachusetts at Amherst. He also teaches courses on Africa at Mount Holyoke College and the University of Massachusetts.

Born in Georgia, Mr. Murphy received his B.A. and M.A. degrees from Emory University in Atlanta, and his Ph.D. from the University of Connecticut. He has taught at Emory University, the University of North Carolina, the University of Connecticut, and the University College of Fort Hare in the Union of South Africa. His academic fields include anthropology, education, history, and sociology.

For seventeen years the author served with the African-American Institute, a major United States private organization working to promote African development and African-American understanding, and for six of those years was its executive vice-president. Mr. Murphy has been a consultant on Africa to the Carnegie Corporation of New York and the Charles F. Kettering Foundation, and on organizational matters to AFS International Scholarships, the Experiment in International Living, and Oxfam-America. He has made numerous trips to most parts of Africa, as well as to Europe and the Pacific Islands. Other books he has written include *The Bantu Civilization of Southern Africa, History of African Civilization, Creative Philanthropy,* and (with Harry Stein) *Teaching Africa Today.*

In his spare time Mr. Murphy is an enthusiastic skier, sailor, and fisherman.

ABOUT THE ILLUSTRATOR

Louise Jefferson's knowledge of African art and culture is the result of extensive travel in Africa, twice on Ford Foundation fellowships and once as a representative of the African-American Institute at a southern African art conference.

A well-known cartographer and calligrapher, Miss Jefferson served for many years as art director with Friendship Press, the publishing dividion of the Missionary Education Movement. She has been a map consultant for the New York State Council for the Arts and a consultant and art coordinator for the New York City Board of Education's special African Project. She has written and illustrated a reference book on the decorative arts of Africa.

Miss Jefferson studied at Howard University, Hunter College and Columbia University. She now lives in Litchfield, Connecticut.